The Landscape of the Mind

The Landscape of the Mind

PASTORALISM AND PLATONIC THEORY
IN TASSO'S *AMINTA* AND
SHAKESPEARE'S EARLY COMEDIES

BY

RICHARD CODY

ὁ φιλόμυθος φιλόσοφός πώς ἐστιν

ARISTOTLE

OXFORD
AT THE CLARENDON PRESS
1969

Oxford University Press, Ely House, London W. 1

GLASGOW NEW YORK TORONTO MELBOURNE WELLINGTON
CAPE TOWN SALISBURY IBADAN NAIROBI LUSAKA ADDIS ABABA
BOMBAY CALCUTTA MADRAS KARACHI LAHORE DACCA
KUALA LUMPUR SINGAPORE HONG KONG TOKYO

PRINTED IN GREAT BRITAIN

TO

MY FATHER AND MOTHER

PREFACE

MY thanks are due to all who have helped me with this book. I should like to acknowledge at least a few of them by name, and above all my wife Violetta. Her voice and hand are in every sentence.

I wish especially to thank Huntington Brown. Six years ago at the University of Minnesota this study, then a doctoral thesis, found in him its first and kindest audience. I have been fortunate in his advice and encouragement ever since. At Minnesota from 1955 to 1961 I was a fellow student of John Fraser's, and the mark of his exceptional mind is on my work. I wish to thank Leo Marx, whose kind interest in the task of turning a thesis into a book goes back to those years.

I am indebted to President Calvin Plimpton and the Trustees of Amherst College and to Louis B. Wright and his staff for summer readerships spent at the British Museum and Folger Shakespeare Libraries in 1963 and 1965. I am also indebted to the librarians of Amherst College for their frequent help.

Over the past three years my colleague G. Armour Craig has often given me insights into literary history and these are reflected in what I have written.

It goes without saying that those I thank here deserve a different book. This one, with all its faults, is the better for my having known the conversation of Theodore Baird.

R. C.

Amherst, Massachusetts
January 1967

ACKNOWLEDGEMENTS

I AM grateful to Richmond Lattimore and the University of Chicago Press for permission to quote from his translation of the *Alcestis* of Euripides, copyright 1955 by the University of Chicago, printed in the *Complete Greek Tragedies,* ed. David Grene and Richmond Lattimore (Chicago, 1959), and to Mr. M. B. Yeats and Messrs. Macmillan and the Macmillan Company of New York for permission to quote the poem *Who Goes With Fergus?* from the *Collected Poems of W. B. Yeats* (London, 1933), copyright 1906 by the Macmillan Company, renewed 1934.

CONTENTS

Translations are by the present author unless otherwise attributed

INTRODUCTION

PASTORALISM AND AESTHETIC
PLATONIC TRADITION

The Scripture affords us a divine pastoral drama in the
Song of Solomon, consisting of two persons and a double
chorus, as Origen rightly judges.

MILTON

(i) *Mythology and Allegory*

THE view of pastoralism offered here is to the best of my knowledge a new one in English studies, but its novelty would not have been evident to the informed audience for poetry from Boccaccio's time to Milton's. It sees the poetic fiction in the customary humanist light as fundamentally allegorical: truth concealed by a known and fitting veil of mythology.[1] And it sees pastoralism as one distinct mode of allegory, of the order, if not the gravity, of the tragic.

Nowadays the pastoral is not usually thought of as a whole phase of the poetic imagination. Even when considered as an aspect of tragi-comedy, its distinctive features are taken to be a stock figure, the shepherd, and the invocation of a Golden Age. What is overlooked in this is that in such a model of Renaissance pastoralism as Tasso's *Aminta* the shepherd is no more important than several other features—the nymph, the satyr, the landscape, the death swoon—and is less important than the manner in which all is turned into a Platonic celebration of the poet's inner life.

What is also overlooked is that the invocation of a Golden Age is less significant than the enactment of a myth of Apollo and Bacchus reconciled, such as the death of Orpheus or the flaying of Marsyas. It is this mythology, and the peculiar self-consciousness with which an audience is invited to respond to it, that in the present essay I consider.

I do not undertake to say how well informed the 'elegant and learned reader', as Milton calls him, actually was in his response to pastoral. To judge by its frequency in the literature of the period this mode made a large and various appeal. And of the modern audience for, say, mystery fiction, how many make the response of

---

[1] G. Boccaccio, *Genealogia Deorum Gentilium*, XIV. vii: 'velamento fabuloso atque decenti veritatem contegere'; J. Milton, *The Reason of Church Government*, ii, preface ,*passim*. Cf. E .Curtius, *Europäische Literatur und lateinisches Mittelalter* (Bern, 1948), Chs. XI, XII.

a Conrad or a Camus, as it may be inferred from what they write? I give only the best account of pastoralism I can after reading two exceptional understanders, Tasso and Shakespeare.

In the late fifteenth century and afterwards the theory that classical mythology concealed the wisdom—and especially the Platonic wisdom—of the ancients was given new force and currency by the Florentine humanists. Pico della Mirandola, for one, several times proposed a treatise on the 'theology' of the Greek and Latin poets. As far as is known this never appeared, but presumably it would have brought together and glossed mythic allusions such as are found in Plato, in Proclus, and in Pico's own master, Ficino—to name only three stages in an exuberant tradition. And prominent among these mythologems or *aenigmatum nodi*, as among the Orphic fragments which Proclus cites, would have been the very elements of pastoral poetry.[1]

From Orpheus, Pythagoras, and Plato a mingled tradition of poetic, religious, and philosophic wisdom was believed by the early Christian Platonists to have come down, dark but pristine, into the new era. And as heirs of the Eastern Empire and its Greek learning the Florentines, too, looked on the 'theology' revealed by Orpheus to Musaeus and on the Socratic Dialogues in one and the same mystical, allegorizing manner.

By virtue of being read as Orphic revelation, the mythology of the *Phaedrus* becomes a model for the pastoral eclogue, as in Pico's commentary on a love poem by Benivieni:

This same chaste love Socrates pursued, who inspired by the beauty

---

[1] Pico della Mirandola, *De Hominis Dignitate . . . e scritti vari*, ed. E. Garin (Florence, 1942), pp. 546, 556, 581 (*Commento sopra una canzona de amore composta da Girolamo Benivieni*); cf. pp. 474–5 (ibid.); pp. 150, 156 (*De Dignitate*); p. 172 (*Heptalus*). For Ficino, cf., e.g., *Opera* (Basle, 1561), ii. 1374 (*In Phaedrum*). For Proclus, cf., e.g., *Orphicorum Fragmenta*, ed. O. Kern (Berlin, 1922), p. 155: ποιμαίνων πραπίδεσσιν ἀνόμματον ὠχὺν ἔρωτα: pasturing in the breast blind, rapid love. Cf. *Orphica*, ed. E. Abel (Leipzig, 1885), p. 89 (Hymn to Eros):

τοξαλκῆ, πτερόεντα, πυρίβρομον, εὔδρομον ὁρμῇ,
συμπαίζοντα θεοῖς ἠδὲ θνητοῖς ἀνθρώποις (ll. 2–3).

Darting and winged, impetuous fierce desire,
With Gods and mortals playing, wand'ring fire.
(Trans. T. Taylor.)

of Phaedrus often times sang beside the river Ilissus the highest mysteries of theology.[1]

In pastoralism the tone of writer and reader alike seems always to have been more or less oracular. Already in the fourteenth century Boccaccio asks who does not see that Virgil in his Eclogues is a philosopher, and quotes the Orphic song of Silenus in support.[2] And now the school of Ficino, whose doctrine is everywhere in the sixteenth century, brings to the reading and writing of pastoral a Platonic sophistication all its own.

The purpose of criticism is to take the poetic fruit and leave the chaff of mere doctrine. But in this case the purpose may be served by recognizing anew that pastoral is esoteric. By keeping in sight its importance as a 'poetic theology' of love, beauty, and the soul— the counterpart, mode for mode, of medieval allegorical romance— a better view of it than usual is to be had, both as an ethos and as a style.

(ii) *Pastoralism and Platonism*

What is the wisdom implicit in Renaissance pastoralism? It would not surprise me to learn that my answer to this question is a commonplace: namely, the Platonic theory of a good inner life, accommodated to the literary myth of the courtier as lover and poet. Stated thus it is certainly a likely answer from the cultural historian's point of view. But if it is a commonplace, it is not one that enjoys much currency.

A reader of literary histories often comes upon the assertion that

---

[1] Pico, ed. Garin, p. 538 (*Commento*). Cf. E. Garin, *G. Pico della Mirandola: vita e dottrina* (Florence, 1937), p. 125 and n.

[2] *Genealogia*, XIV. x. Cf. J. Seznec, *La Survivance des dieux antiques* (London, 1940), pp. 88–90, 187–93. Boccaccio follows Petrarch, as in *Le familiari*, ed. V. Rossi (Florence, 1933), ii. 304, who asserts the properly cryptic nature of all pastoral language: 'id genus est quod, nisi ipso qui condidit auditum, intelligi non possit' (x. 4): this kind of composition is such that, unless one has heard the author's explanation, it is not able to be understood. Cf. *Epistolae Variae*, ed. J. Fracassetti (Florence, 1863), iii. 410–11 (XLII). Also Virgil, *Bucolics*, ii. 4: 'ibi haec *incondita* solus . . .': there alone [fling to the hills and woods] these artless strains (Loeb trans.).

pastoralism, and especially the pastoral play, is a characteristic expression of the Renaissance poetic mind. But satisfying explanations of this are more difficult to come by—William Empson's studies in verbal ambiguity aside. The pastoral play is virtually invented by Poliziano around 1480; without mentioning him Guarini acknowledges as much in the *Compendium of Tragi-Comic Poetry*. Yet how can the mean and narrow world of the shepherd, as Schiller calls it (*enge dürftige Hirtenwelt*), be characteristic of the rich, expansive imagination of the Renaissance? Empson explains the paradox, inimitably, as political wordplay: putting the complex into the simple for a class purpose. Is it not also to be explained as philosophic mythopoeia?

Pastoralism may be the poetic expression *par excellence* of that cult of aesthetic Platonism which arose in Florence at the same moment and spread across Europe during the next half century. In England aesthetic Platonism was introduced at its best by Erasmus and More, and found its first influential poetic voice in Spenser— though the subtle humours of the *Praise of Folly* or *Utopia* and the 'high sentence' of the *Faerie Queene* speak for an exceptional variety of style in this tradition.[1]

But suppose this were so—and mythology, as Aristotle says, a form of philosophy—where in Renaissance studies is the evidence for any special connection between Platonism and pastoralism? Cassirer in his *Platonic Renaissance in England* has no more to say about the one than Greg in *Pastoral Poetry and Pastoral Drama* has to say about the other. The fact that both traditions coincide in the work of certain key figures—Virgil, Boethius, Petrarch, Cervantes, Blake, Goethe—is hardly conclusive.

Some more than accidental connection begins to appear when one notices the mutual concerns of the two traditions in their Renaissance phase. There is the claim of contemplation against the active life, typical of pastoral and of such products of the Florentine circle as Landino's *Disputationes Camaldulenses*. And there are the common themes of love and poetry, Eros and Logos, as developed

---

[1] E. Cassirer, *Die platonische Renaissance in England und die Schule von Cambridge* (Leipzig, 1932), pp. 8–17, 74–82.

in Ficino's own *Commentarium in Convivium Platonis*, a debate that shows how heavy the Careggian air was with the *Symposium*.

Then there is the hermetic reading of mythology which gives rise to a poetic language common to syncretizing Platonists like Pico, Leone Ebreo, or Bruno, and to pastoral artists of all kinds— Botticelli, Michelangelo, Titian, as well as Poliziano, Sannazaro, Tasso. And finally there is that peculiar interior yet sensuous mood, compounded of idealism, the aesthetic, Eros, and reminiscence, which is easier to recognize in both traditions than to define.

This is not the point at which to develop a detailed answer on the doctrine found in pastoralism, but one piece of evidence will serve as well to urge the question. It is from Ficino's second commentary on the *Philebus*, where his remarks on the judgement of Paris open as follows:

> Paris, the son of an eastern king, pastures his flock in a wood: that is, the soul created by God delights with the senses in the material confusion of the elements. Three goddesses, Pallas, Juno, Venus, offer themselves to him for judgement as forms of transcendent beauty.[1]

The story is a familiar one, and Paris as he figures in it is a recognized type of the Renaissance shepherd.[2] But what is of interest is Ficino's reading of the pastoral mythology.

In its aesthetic rather than ethical or cosmological tradition, Platonism always seeks to comprehend in a single formula the dualism of a 'delight in the sensible universe' and a 'beatific vision of divine perfection'. These phrases are from Lovejoy's *Great Chain of Being*, but Cassirer puts the same matter more fully in the *Individual and Cosmos* with particular reference to Ficino's theory of Eros. For Ficino the attraction for man of the divine is explained only by the reciprocal attraction for God of the human and natural. Thus Eros is conceived of as a mutual desire of the intelligible for the sensual and the lower being for the higher, as transcendental yet immanent.

Now is not pastoralism an allegorical expression of some such

---

[1] *Supplementum Ficinianum*, ed. P. O. Kristeller (Florence, 1937), i. 80.
[2] H. Smith, *Elizabethan Poetry* (Cambridge, Mass., 1952), pp. 3–9.

religious consciousness as this, some new 'culture of the sensible world'? Is not Ficino's reading of the Paris myth the doctrinal equivalent of what a pastoral poet also seeks to do? Does not the symbolic mental landscape and ambiguous language of pastoral typically seek to comprehend an erotic dualism of 'this-worldliness' and 'otherworldliness'?[1]

Long before Hallett Smith put Paris forward as the type of the Renaissance shepherd, Symonds had done the same for Orpheus, the personification of a reviving antique culture, a new Arcadia.[2] And there is ample evidence in the art of the period for either view. Given the paraphrastic quality of all mythic thinking, a plurality of heroes is to be expected. And common to Paris and Orpheus, and confirming their final identity for the Platonizing thinker or poet, there is the role they both play in mythic paradigms of the One and the Many.

The One and the Many is rationalism's way of naming the mystery that lies behind myths like the judgement of Paris—of which the death of Orpheus and the dismemberment of Bacchus are accordingly analogues. How, after all, ought shepherd Paris to have chosen? Monism, as William James drily observes, has usually kept itself vague and mystical as regards the ultimate principle of unity.[3] But no doubt Paris ought, like Orpheus, to have reconciled his immanental erotic perception of the Many in some transcendent concept of the One. You favour all three goddesses equally, Ficino tells Lorenzo de' Medici in a letter about the *summum bonum* of the *Philebus*. The mystery is how.

The same monistic formula applies to Orpheus, not as sacred victim but as theologian, in the following passsage from Pico:

... why Love, of all the gods, is by Orpheus placed in the bosom of Chaos is because Chaos means nothing other than matter, full of all the forms, but confused and imperfect ...[4]

[1] E. Cassirer, *Individuum und Kosmos in der Philosophie der Renaissance* (Leipzig, 1927), p. 140. Cf. *Platonische Renaissance*, pp. 66–74; A. O. Lovejoy, *The Great Chain of Being* (Cambridge, Mass., 1936), p. 316.

[2] J. A. Symonds, *Renaissance in Italy* (London, 1907), IV. ii. 192.

[3] W. James, *Some Problems of Philosophy* (New York, 1911), pp. 115–16.

[4] Pico, ed. Garin, p. 504 (*Commento*).

Everywhere in Platonic theory and pastoral mythology love brings forth the manifold beauty of things and yet leads back to the invisible unity of God, as most evidently in Botticelli's *Primavera*, a distinctive *poesia* of the Florentine circle. Pico expresses the same perennial concern with a vision of unity as the prerequisite of true perception when he enigmatically affirms:

> Whoever cannot attract Pan will have approached Nature and Proteus in vain.[1]

Here, in the Orphic *Conclusiones*, pastoral language again veils a Platonic mystery of the One found in the Many.

(iii) *Scholarship and Criticism*

All the secondary evidence I can adduce in support of this view of pastoralism is a handful of studies in cultural history and classical philology. The most familiar is that brilliant first essay of the generation before Greg's, Nietzsche's *Birth of Tragedy*. Nietzsche is there most concerned with Greek tragedy and German opera, and the notice he takes of Renaissance pastoralism is passing and contemptuous. But implicit in the account of the birth of tragedy from the spirit of music is a unique essay on the birth of pastoral from the spirit of Socratic Platonism.

In the eighth chapter there comes a brief reference to the idyllic shepherd of the modern age as the descendant of the choric satyr of antiquity. This divinity, says Nietzsche, is the embryo of a tragic mode which passes from its maturity in Aeschylus to its decadence in Euripides—thanks to the cheerful and temperate influence of Socrates. Now if pastoralism is indeed the post-Euripidean, pre-operatic decadence of the tragic mode, how would Nietzsche's mythopoeic theory of Greek tragedy illuminate it?

The divinity which spoke through Euripides was neither Dionysos nor Apollo, but a brand new daemon called Socrates.[2]

[1] Pico, *Opera* (Basle, 1557), p. 107.
[2] F. Nietzsche, *Die Geburt der Tragödie* (Stuttgart, 1955), p. 110 (trans. F. Golffing).

Is the Alexandrian art of pastoral thus a latter-day Socratic plot to revive and reconcile the gods of tragedy in some new non-tragic mode?

If one entertains this thesis that Nietzsche hardly bothered to develop, then the connection between pastoralism and aesthetic Platonism begins to look implicit in other cultural historians as well. Burckhardt, though he prefers the bucolic to be lifelike, still sees that the making of even Flemish fifteenth-century landscape art is a quality he calls 'soul' (*Seele*). Huizinga says clearly that what defines Renaissance pastoral and relates it to the chivalric is erotic idealism. Leonardo Olschki allows one to infer a Platonic rationale for pastoralism from his remarks on courtly love, Eros, and Italian drama in the sixteenth century. And Curtius, in tracing back the motif of ideal landscape to its origins, pointedly juxtaposes the *Idylls* of Theocritus and the *Phaedrus*.[1]

It is Adam Parry, however, in a notable essay on landscape in Greek poetry, who once and for all makes the connection explicit:

> Plato, though never a pastoral writer in the strict sense, seems to have been its originator.[2]

And the confirmation comes in Bruno Snell's essay on Greek poetry and philosophy called the *Discovery of the Mind*. It is significant for the study of pastoralism in all its phases that this account of the development of the Greek mind from Homer through Plato ends with Virgil's invention of the spiritual landscape (*geistige Landschaft*) of Arcadia.

In the *Bucolics* the Greek mind, fully self-conscious but able to speak of itself only in metaphor, finds its first classic expression in European art. In the Tenth Eclogue in particular, where the love passion, the beauty of nature, and the solace of art (Gallus, Pan, Apollo) are given a single voice, pastoralism becomes the model in which the Greek mind can be imitated by the artists of the Middle Ages and Renaissance, both as myth and as style.

---

[1] Curtius, p. 193. Cf. J. Burckhardt, *Gesammelte Werke* (Basle, 1955), iii. 202–3; J Huizinga, *Men and Ideas*, trans. J. S. Holmes and H. van Marle (New York, 1959), p. 85; L. Olschki, *La poesia italiana del Cinquecento* (Florence, 1933), pp. 25–32, 41–6.

[2] A. Parry, 'Landscape in Greek Poetry', *Yale Classical Studies*, xv (1957), 29.

This model, as Snell points out, has no counterpart in previous Greek poetry, being a self-contained form of beauty whose reality is in itself; art as symbol. But what comes nearest to it, as an anticipation, is the myth-making of Plato in the Dialogues. Plato's myths are not, like Virgil's, self-contained, since they refer to arguments he would present rationally if he had the language to do so. For this reason he deprecates them as mere play—again in anticipation of the pastoralist.[1]

Snell also finds antecedents of the *Bucolics* in the mythological plays which epitomize the influence of Socratic Platonism on poetry, those of Euripides. And when he looks for an Arcadia like Virgil's he finds it, not so much in the ostensible model, Theocritus, as in the Platonic Academy, that island of the contemplative life where the arch-mythologer retired in search of an ambience in which the question 'What is Justice?' could be pursued:

Iam redit et Virgo, redeunt Saturnia regna.[2]

(*Bucolics* iv. 6)

Ficino, incidentally, sees the same analogy in reverse when he reads the landscape or *locus amoenus* in the *Phaedrus* as an allegory of the Academic life; a tradition which Milton also observes:

See there the Olive Grove of Academe.

(*Paradise Regained*, iv. 244)

For Ficino, however, it is the plane tree (*platanus*), not the olive, that punningly clinches this allegorical reading.[3]

The trick of seeing into pastoralism, one may conclude, is not to allow any of its details, such as the shepherd's life, to limit the view, but to look for meaning and value in perspectives of one's own choosing.

(iv) *The* Aminta *and the Early Comedies*

In reading the *Aminta* I find that what best illuminates its pastoralism is Florentine poetic theology. This is no doubt partly

[1] B. Snell, *Die Entdeckung des Geistes* (Hamburg, 1955), p. 399.
[2] Now too returns the virgin [Astraea, or Justice], the reign of Saturn returns.
[3] Ficino, ii. 1363, 1373 (*In Phaedrum*). Cf. H. Petriconi, 'Das neue Arkadien', *Antike und Abendland*, iii (1946), 199.

because Florentine doctrine remains current right through Tasso's
lifetime and is highly eclectic into the bargain. But it is also because
Ficino and Pico are at times consciously Orphic writers, which
brings them on to common ground with the pastoralist.

Yet even the pure Platonism of the *Symposium* and *Phaedrus*
throws more light on Tasso's pastoralism than one might think.
Indeed, a rationale for the whole mode of literature which the
Aminta epitomizes may be inferred from that famous conversation
mentioned at the end of the *Symposium* where Socrates argues for
the poet who can write both tragedy and comedy. And in the
Phaedrus the essential pastoral myth of Apollo and Bacchus reconciled
is made explicit when he argues—in shepherd's guise if ever
cultivated man was—that the truest art is to live naturally. Both
the ethos and the style of pastoral find classic definition here, as
Socratic optimism and as *discordia concors*, the mythologer's equivalent of paradox.

In the Italian Renaissance, in a Platonizing culture dominated by
the courtly ethos, pastoralism becomes the temper of the aristo-
cratic mind: the reconciling of discords and contradictions in the
medium of the work of art, that shadow of the ideal. The message
of pastoralism, communicated on the image level, as it has been
called, is this: that this-worldliness and otherworldliness can be
reconciled, and that a truly cultivated man, whatever his intimations
of divinity, may find a natural human voice. The burden of the
pastoral poet, however lightly felt, is thus an enactment of the
Socratic compromise between artifice and naturalness, transcendence and immanence.

Orthodox Italian pastoralism brings together the psychology of
human love and the mysteries of Neo-Platonic theology in a celebration of the poet's own art. This the *Aminta* serves to establish.
In its mythological *intermedi*, which I find are integral to the
shepherd love plot, there is clearly enacted a serial reconciliation
of Apollo and Bacchus: 'kinaesthesis and vision—the . . . typical
ingredients of the human situation at whatever level of advancement'.[1] Here delight in the sensible universe again seeks by

---

[1] P. Wheelwright, *The Burning Fountain* (Bloomington, 1954), p. 157.

means of mythological language to become a beatific vision of divine perfection. Tasso's concern as a mythologer is thus explicitly that of his antique predecessors in the satyr play and in tragedy, except that the dramatic ceremony has become, as Nietzsche saw, tragi-comic, doctrinaire Neo-Platonic, and self-consciously aesthetic—in a word, pastoral.

Once the poetic identity of Platonism and pastoralism as in the *Aminta* is recognized, then the possibility arises that Shakespeare's so-called romantic comedies are in some related sense pastoral. It is chiefly Cassirer's omission of all but these from detailed discussion in his survey of the Platonic Renaissance in England that confirms as much. *Love's Labour's Lost*, one might say, is his token and preferred instance of Elizabethan aesthetic Platonism under its pastoral-comical aspect. The insight of his praise of this play makes up for his silence about any more orthodox work in the same mode. And outside Shakespeare, what comparable English pastoral is there?

Tasso's *Aminta*, in spite of its deadly reputation as a classic, is a good enough piece of poetry and drama to bear comparison with Shakespeare's early comedies. This is especially true of that mythological language of allusion in which the pastoral mysteries are expressed. In his Platonism and his use of the poetic theology Tasso is much the more doctrinaire of the two. And his control of the tone and rhythm of plot as well as language is less interesting because less experimental. But the advantage of recognizing that the orthodox, elegiac Italian and the festive English comedian speak a common language of pastoral Neo-Platonism is considerable.

Not that anybody nowadays is going to be much moved by intimations of Eros and Logos, even in Shakespeare. But by comparing what as pastoralists he and Tasso do with language one can see into a certain stage of the coming to consciousness of Renaissance poetry—a stage which anticipates that 'unmasking of previous symbolisms' so much to be admired in Jonson, Donne, and their schools.[1] And one can also see that in this case, even as it becomes more and more clearly recognized as rhetoric and not

[1] E. Jones, 'Theory of Symbolism', cited in E. H. Gombrich, *Meditations on a Hobby Horse* (London, 1963), p. 30.

religion, poetry never quite gives up its old power as a ritual language of the mysteries, validated by myths that are sacred. This may explain, as de Rougemont suggests, why the courtly-love myth of which pastoralism is part retains such a hold over the European imagination long after entering its purely literary phase.[1]

(v) *Iconography and Orphism*

It is the scholarly findings of the last few decades in Renaissance iconology which make a comparison of Tasso's and Shakespeare's pastoral styles feasible. A vocabulary of terms has been defined, mythological in reference but by implication Platonic, which is common to the writers as well as to the plastic artists of the period. Edgar Wind in his chapter on the relation of Proteus to Pan identifies a term of the poetic theology which is also important in the pastoralism of the *Aminta* and the *Two Gentlemen of Verona*.[2] Erwin Panofsky in *Hercules at the Crossways*, by his account of this pastoral (*verlandschaftlicht*) motif in a painting of Raphael's, incidentally clarifies *Love's Labour's Lost*. And to these names should be added that of E. H. Gombrich for his part in bringing a knowledge of Platonic aestheticism to bear in the reading of sixteenth-century mythological styles.

Of all the mythic figures in the poetic theology Orpheus is the one most important to pastoralism. Besides the richness of his myth, which is exceptional, there is the canon of writings with which he is eponymously credited. The invocation of his name in an appropriate context of love, landscape, and poetry can be said to signalize the Renaissance pastoral mode. It is, for example, the clue to a conscious community which exists among Poliziano in the *Orfeo*, Tasso in the *Aminta*, Shakespeare in *A Midsummer-Night's Dream*, and Milton in *L'Allegro* and *Il Penseroso*, *Comus*, and *Lycidas*.

In Shakespeare's case this clue is not emphatic but still significant:

> 'The riot of the tipsy Bacchanals,
> Tearing the Thracian singer in their rage,'
> That is an old device. . . . (*AMND*, v. i. 48–50)

[1] D. de Rougemont, *L'Amour et l'Occident* (Paris, 1939), pp. 236–7.
[2] E. Wind, *Pagan Mysteries in the Renaissance* (London, 1958), Ch. XIII.

It is curious, as A. W. Ward long since noted, that this remark given to Theseus should seem to be directed at a play such as Poliziano's. And it is equally curious that in the topical allusion which follows it, the death alluded to is, as Chambers says, apparently Tasso's:[1]

> 'The thrice three Muses mourning for the death
> of learning, late deceased in beggary.' (v. i. 52–3)

As so often in certain of the early comedies, the tone of both these allusions is that special one of humorous, quasi-Orphic initiation:

> Where more is meant than meets the ear. (*Il Penseroso*, l. 120)

The fable that Theseus after all prefers to those of Orpheus and the other darling of the Muses is the Pyramus and Thisbe. And in so far as this is a burlesque epitome of the entire plot which it brings to a close, Shakespeare may be understood to say with some deprecation that his own fabling is Orphic, too.

But a more cogent reason than this can be found for considering *A Midsummer-Night's Dream* as the third of his early experiments in pastoral comedy. It is that there are few more useful glosses on its mysterious language of night and dreams, Diana-Luna-Hecate, Apollo, Venus, and so on, than Thomas Taylor's annotated version of the Orphic hymns, published in 1787.

This little book makes as curious reading as most of Ficino or Pico, since it soberly discusses the familiar classical allusions of English poetry as Neo-Platonic doctrine. All of them, it assumes, are Orphic mythologems and, as such, esoteric metaphors for aspects of a solar deity whose light and dark phases are respectively Apollo and Bacchus. But it serves the same purpose as Ficino, or Macrobius in the *Saturnalia*, or the Orphica itself, in recalling a whole cosmos of fine fabling once known to every 'elegant and learned reader' but now largely ignored.

I mention Taylor's book in preference to his chief authority, Proclus, because Shakespeare could not possibly have read it, however much his Latin and Greek. For my argument is not that

[1] A. W. Ward, *History of English Dramatic Literature* (New York, 1899), ii. 381 n.; E. K. Chambers, *William Shakespeare* (Oxford, 1930), i. 360.

Shakespeare knew any such source of the poetic theology as the
Orphica or its commentators—though the hymns alone went
through more than a dozen editions during the sixteenth century.
It was not necessary for him to know them. What, after all, is
Orphism but classical mythology understood as a religious mystery?[1]

That Shakespeare knew the mythology is evident. That the
allegorical theory of poetry was too commonplace for him not
to know is unquestionable. And the presence of a 'theological'
allegory in poetry like Ovid's is plainly canvassed by his English
contemporaries:

> It sufficeth me therefore to note this, that the men of greatest
> learning and highest wit in ancient times did of purpose conceal these
> deep mysteries of learning . . . that they might not be rashly abused by
> profane wits . . . for conservation of the memory of their precepts . . .
> and to be able with one kind of meat and one dish (as I may so call it)
> to feed divers tastes. For the weaker capacities will feed themselves
> with the pleasantness of the history and sweetness of the verse, some
> that have stronger stomachs will as it were take a further taste of
> the moral sense, a third sort more high conceited than they will
> digest the allegory. . . .[2]

This is Harington in his preface to the *Orlando furioso*, but it could
be any Elizabethan critic from Lodge and Sidney on, or any Italian
after Boccaccio. For this, in large measure, *is* the Renaissance
defence of poetry as fable: a *naïveté* on which the sophisticated
mythological language of Tasso and Shakespeare and their contemporaries paradoxically rests.

I do not suppose that Shakespeare thought of himself as a
Platonist, or of his early comedies as Orphic, any more than
Conrad thought of himself as an Existentialist or of the *Secret Agent*
as *série noire*. And no doubt the author of *Hamlet* would have smiled
at the term 'pastoral-comical'. But for the reader who knows
something of these related esoteric traditions—the Platonic, the
Orphic, and the pastoral—a certain quality in his comic language

---

[1] I. M. Linforth, *The Arts of Orpheus* (Berkeley, 1941), pp. 236–42; D. P. Walker,
'Orpheus the Theologian and Renaissance Platonists', *Journal of the Warburg and
Courtauld Institutes*, xvi (1953), 103.

[2] *Elizabethan Critical Essays*, ed. G. G. Smith (Oxford, 1904), ii. 202–3.

comes to light which would otherwise remain obscure. *Qui habet aures audiendi audiat.*

(vi) *Wit and Humour*

What Shakespeare brings to pastoral tradition is not a combination of formality and passion, as in the *Aminta*, but a rich and unique variation on the Platonic sense of humour. A certain humour has always informed pastoral language, a spirit not of laughter but of play—*facetiae*—which is no less apt for tragedy than for the comic. And it is this which Shakespeare may be seen modifying with his own peculiar liberality in the *Two Gentlemen of Verona* and *Love's Labour's Lost.*

The 'civil war of wits' in Euphuistic plays like these finds its solvent in a humour which is the clear contrary of the divisive, the dogmatic, and the puritanical. As Cassirer so well observes, it is a form of Platonic optimism, to which deeper perceptions of men and things than those in the early comedies are also open. This I take to be the humour whose mode in poetry and drama is traditionally pastoral: that *äesthetische Sokratismus* which Nietzsche identifies as the spirit of both Euripides and Mozart. But in Shakespeare the Platonism and the pastoralism are present only as a self-contained mythopoeia, the doctrine all embodied in the self-justifying serio-comic style—a tendency which aesthetic tradition has shown ever since Plato.

In *A Midsummer-Night's Dream*, accordingly, there emerges a poetic language which has its ideal and sceptical elements integrated in a single humorous mode of perception: a pastoralism so freely modified as to cease being evidently pastoral at all. Yet it still follows the pastoral rhythm of dramatic action, still echoes, if mockingly, the 'theology' of the Platonists, and still seeks a reconciliation of divisions in the courtly mind through the ceremony of the living word. So it still asks to be recognized as the pastoralism it no longer quite is.

Such a view of the early comedies sees Shakespeare as an heir of Erasmus in the *Praise of Folly*. The humour of that remarkable piece of prose overruns the limit of anything that can usefully be called pastoralism. But in doing so it draws attention to how much they have in common. There is the aesthetic Socratism of Erasmus's mythological language of Apollo, Bacchus, Pan, and so on. And there is the liberal Christian classicism of his *serio ludere* on the topic of the good inner life. The allegorical language of *discordia concors*— a conceited wit and a humour of mythopoeic reconciliation—is as clearly to be seen in the *Praise of Folly* under its Erasmian species as in the *Aminta* and the early comedies under two others. And if there is less to be said of Shakespeare's Christianity and classicism than of Erasmus's, this is partly because he is more the complete and autonomous pastoral poet.

In the light of the *Praise of Folly* one more question concerning pastoralism may be raised. It concerns its relation to Christian as well as Platonic tradition. If Platonism is indeed the informing philosophy of pastoral literature from its Greek origins to the Renaissance and after, then does this not explain the special acceptability of an apparently foolish fiction to serious Christian poets like Spenser and Milton, as well as to more sceptical ones like Tasso and Shakespeare? For it would then be a poetry of that universal theism on the Platonic model ('wahrhaft universellen Auffassung vom *Logos* selbst') which was recommended all over Europe in the writings of Christian humanists like Ficino and Erasmus.[1]

In Shakespeare this syncretic idealism on the Erasmian model becomes further compromised by a sceptical naturalism—though not so severely as in Montaigne. On the verge of its breakdown, discourse of reason in the aesthetic Platonic manner takes the form of an inspired Shakespearian wisdom of courtly folly: a pastoral idiom which the poet of *Comus* and *Lycidas* was never for all his Italian studies quite to command.

It is in the early comedies and their pastoral *serio ludere* that English poetry finds its most satisfying expression of the moral value of unseriousness. Or, to put the point another way, it is in

[1] Cassirer, *Platonische Renaissance*, p. 14; Seznec, p. 90. Cf. D. P. Walker, 'The *Prisca Theologia* in France', *Journal of the Warburg and Courtauld Institutes*, xvii (1954), 204–59.

their aesthetic wisdom that Renaissance pastoral drama in English
makes its best contribution to the liberalizing of the European mind.

(vii) *Doctrine*

It remains to acknowledge my evident debt to Edgar Wind's
invaluable *Pagan Mysteries in the Renaissance*—a debt as great as I owe
to the other *sine qua non* of this essay, Cassirer's *Platonic Renaissance*—
and to mention that no more specifically literary studies of aesthetic
Platonic tradition in England seem to exist. I do not mean surveys
or monographs on what the Elizabethans knew about Platonism
and mythology—these have been undertaken—but critical studies
of the bearing of this knowledge on their poetic modes and language.
Eliot's essays on Senecan tradition are a notable instance of such
studies in the case of tragedy.

For if a certain Platonic and pastoral mode of poetry is, as I
suggest, common to Tasso and Shakespeare, then at present there
is as little documentation of this as of what Theocritus and Virgil
share in as pastoralists: 'Through the Alexandrian period there is,
as we know, no traceable continuity from the Greek poets to
Virgil. And if the latter opted for certain themes, guided by his
own preoccupations, what does this lack of continuity matter, so
long as a filiation is apparent to us?'[1] Thus Jacqueline Duchemin in
her study of the pastoral origins of Greek poetry. In the absence
of a study of the continuity of the poetic theology in sixteenth-
century literature, this is the very assumption on which the
present comparison of Tasso and Shakespeare must proceed.

[1] J. Duchemin, *La Houlette et la lyre* (Paris, 1960), i. 44.

I

THE PASTORALISM OF
TASSO'S *AMINTA*

1

THE ORPHIC VOICE

... τὴν ἀρετὴν ἔχειν τι πάντως καὶ σατυρικὸν μέρος ...

PLUTARCH

(i) Socrates and Orpheus

To see that the *Aminta*, like so much else in Renaissance art and letters, is a footnote to Plato, one should come to it by way of the *Phaedrus* and Poliziano's *Orfeo*. These are the loci of this chapter: Socratic speech and Orphic song. Poliziano's is the earliest play in the same mode as Tasso's, but Plato in his prose idyll anticipates much of their common manner and matter. It is the voice of Socrates that in Italian pastoral, under the influence of Ficino, emerges as Orphic.

What makes for this affiliation is the persistence from Plato's time through Ficino's of an aesthetic theory of the inner life. Contemplation is 'transposed' by Plato, scholarship being given an intelligible object, and religion a divine one whose beauty is visible only to the soul. The effort is in either case the same, to live the life of reason by transcending existential emotion: 'pour amener à une vue plus intérieure et plus pure'.[1] In the Dialogues the exhortation to this life is spoken by Socrates, a hero true to himself who, like Orpheus, never quite dies.

A concern with withdrawal into the self, self-examination, and a discovery of beauty by the same creative process as the poet's remains the mark of aesthetic Platonism through Plotinus and Cusanus to Ficino and the School of Cambridge.[2] On occasion, therefore, Plato and Ficino's fellow academic Poliziano conform to

---

[1] A.-J. Festugière, *Contemplation et vie contemplative selon Platon* (Paris, 1950), p. 73.
[2] Cassirer, *Platonische Renaissance*, pp. 19–20; *Individuum und Kosmos*, p. 143.

a single mode of composition: a verbal art of landscape which is an allegory of the inner life.

To temper the mind by putting it into terms of landscape and its gods, and of verbal wit and humour—this is the pastoral and Orphic action of the *Phaedrus*. In the *Symposium*, it is said, 'we see with Plato's eyes the interior life of the soul of Socrates', while in the *Phaedrus* he gives us 'a fuller description of the working of passion in the individual soul'.[1]

Socrates and his disciple, a 'pattern of Golden Age simplicity', retire from Athens to the countryside along the Ilissus. The spot they come to is natural, delightful, but not uncultivated: a plane tree and willow stand on rising ground, a spring flows, and sacred statues are visible among the grasses. Here the two philologues discuss how to write or talk well about love.

The spot reminds Phaedrus of the rape of Oreithyia by Boreas, which supposedly occurred near by, and he raises the question of how such myths are to be interpreted. Socrates answers:

> I investigate not these things but myself, to know whether I am a monster more complicated and more furious than Typhon or a gentler and simpler creature to whom a divine and quiet lot is given by nature. (230, Loeb trans.)

In so far as this account of discord in the soul implies a remedy, it is the pastoral art of 'putting the complex into the simple', and one in which the art of poetry itself is epitomized.[2] But what remains intrinsic to the dialectic here, and so to the virtue of self-knowledge, is the very language of myth which Socrates does not investigate, mythology being a means not of discrimination but analogy.

Socrates makes clear from the first that he is a man of the city and that 'country places and trees' will teach him nothing compared with people. Accordingly, his speeches on the divinity of love involve the landscape and Pan, Apollo, Dionysos, the Muses, and Aphrodite only 'in some sort of figurative manner'—as allegory

---

[1] A. E. Taylor, *Plato* (London, 1927), p. 225; G. Grube, *Plato's Thought* (London, 1935), p. 113.

[2] W. Empson, *Some Versions of Pastoral* (London, 1935), p. 23. Cf. *Seven Types of Ambiguity* (London, 1947), p. 114.

(265B). On the other hand, his unfailing piety towards love and language makes him pious about myth as well.

So before leaving the delightful spot he prays to its gods, again on the theme of unity in the soul:

O beloved Pan and all ye other gods of this place, grant me that I may be made beautiful in my soul within, and that all my external possessions be in harmony with my inner man. (279B)

With pastoralism there is usually this cult of enigma. The voice in which the Delphic virtue is vested tries to comprehend both the urbane and the naïve, the ironic and the pious. Like the Ion whom Plutarch cites, its teaching is that virtue should always, as in tragic drama, have its satyric side.[1]

In the *Phaedrus*, as in an Italian pastoral play, Eros impends throughout, binding all being into a cosmos, making converse possible between gods and men, and moving the philosopher or poet to utterance. Inspiration is by definition passionate and maniacal. Procreation matters little as compared with creativity in the soul. And for all the sense of beauty, the physical is treated as a life to be transcended—a noetic impulse which Socrates elsewhere identifies as Orphic (*Cratylus*, 400C).

The love of which he is sick is love of discourse, a deliberate sublimation of natural and moral impulse in the medium of words. Yet he dismisses written discourse as 'sportive jest':

The man who thinks that . . . no written discourse, whether in metre or in prose, deserves to be treated seriously . . .—that man, Phaedrus, is likely to be such as you and I might pray we may become. (277E–278B)

If part of the greatness of Plato is 'to have confessed that there are certain ultimate truths which it is beyond the powers of human reason to demonstrate scientifically', then this is the putative virtue of the pastoralist also—a sophisticated self-deprecation.[2] Much of the guileless amateur manner of pastoralism, as combined

---

[1] Plutarch, *Pericles*, v. Cf. *Symposium*, 215–17, Alcibiades' praise of Socrates as a Silenus or Marsyas.

[2] W. K. C. Guthrie, *Orpheus and Greek Religion* (London, 1952), p. 239.

with a highly conscious artifice, is to be found here and in Socrates' earlier assertion that with sportive words 'one who knows the truth may lead his readers on' (262D). This is the credo of an esoteric. 'Neither tell I you by what authority I do these things' (Matt. 21: 27).

But is the pastoralism of the *Orfeo* and *Aminta* wholly anticipated in the *Phaedrus*? And would Plato recognize this as a distinct mode of composition at all?

The Arcadian *personae* and the pursuit of the nymph, which Poliziano and Tasso make much of, are all but absent. The patenting of these is the work of two conscious pastoralists: Virgil, who 'does not mention Plato's name but was a follower of his',[1] and Ovid, whose mythologies amply make up for any frugality of motifs in the *Phaedrus*. And although Socrates singles out for praise the man (like Orpheus) of a 'musical and loving nature', his crucial myth of life in the soul is quite unpastoral—that of the charioteer and two winged horses.

The point cannot be, then, that this Dialogue is the unique source of pastoral mythopoeia. It must rather be that Plato's invention of the voice of Socrates—at once dramatic and mythic, rational and mystical—makes him a felt presence behind any such 'plausible discourse' on love in a landscape as the *Orfeo*, the *Aminta*, or Shakespeare's early comedies.

As for his recognizing the *Phaedrus* as pastoral, the question is academic since Ficino and Pico evidently did so. But Plato does seem to have distinguished such a mode, in poetry if not prose. In the *Ion*, during the account of poetic inspiration, Socrates differentiates between the 'ring' of Homer and that of Orpheus, which would correspond to the heroic and pastoral respectively (536B). Milton makes a similar distinction in the invocations of *Paradise Lost*.[2]

---

[1] F. Petrarca, *De Sui Ipsius et Multorum Ignorantia*, ed. L. Capelli (Paris, 1906), p. 72. Cf. H. More, *Philosophical Writings* (London, 1712), p. 77 (*Conjectura Cabbalistica*): 'that excellent Platonist Virgil'.

[2] iii. 17-18; ix. 14-15. In so far as Milton speaks of his epic voice as a nightingale (iii. 37-40), the Homeric can be understood to comprehend the Orphic. According to Pausanias, the nightingale that nests on the tomb of Orpheus sings more sweetly and louder than any others (*Description of Greece*, IX. xxx. 6).

If the *Phaedrus* is pastoral, are there not features of the same mode to be found in the theatre of Plato's time? Guarini, author of the *Pastor fido* and a determined neo-classicist, does not think so:

Although the *favola pastorale* finds its origin, as to persons introduced, in the eclogue and satyr play of the ancients, nevertheless, as to form and order it may be called a modern invention, since no such fable is found in Greek or Latin.[1]

But when it suits his argument he will mention that in the *Oedipus* of Sophocles it is the shepherds who bring on the denouement. It may be that there is no pastoral proper in the classical theatre simply because the tragic, with its satyric part, is itself pastoral. And one may wonder if in Euripides, the favourite of Renaissance Hellenists, there is not at times something very like pastoral drama to be seen supplanting the tragic.

The *Alcestis* in particular, besides introducing Apollo in bucolic retreat at Pherae, answers to a mood which is serious without being tragic and comic without being laughable. There is also the *Cyclops*, a satyric laugh-raiser, and the *Bacchae*, a high tragedy of maenadism. All anticipate the *Orfeo* and *Aminta* in something, if only the satyr figure. Yet not even the *Alcestis*, with its proto-pastoral ethos of love, loss, longing, self-transcendence and reconciliation in life, has anything like the Italianate mood of sensuous inwardness.

Any affinity of Euripides' tragi-comedy with the *favola pastorale* may be traced to what the Alcestis myth has in common with the myth of Orpheus. The two are mentioned together by Plato as famous proofs of the power of love over death, and like most of his references to Orpheus this has an important bearing on the development of pastoralism as a love allegory.

It is Phaedrus who in the *Symposium* cites Alcestis as a lover whose readiness to die for her husband induces the gods to release her soul temporarily from Hades. Nothing is said of the roles of Apollo and the satyric Hercules in this undoing of death. All turns on the ardour of the selfless lover. Orpheus, on the other hand, is

<hr />

[1] G. Guarini, *Compendio della poesia tragicomica*, ed. G. Brognoligo (Bari, 1914), pp. 271–2. Cf. M. Bieber, *History of the Greek and Roman Theatre* (Princeton, 1939), p. 24.

disparaged. He is a cowardly minstrel who lacked the courage to die for his love and entered Hades alive. For this reason he was cheated by the gods with a mere shadow of Eurydice, which disappeared, and he was fated to die at the hands of women (179D).

Such a reading of the myth is unusual, for the Dialogues or anywhere else. In the *Alcestis*, when Admetus laments that he has neither the voice nor the music to charm the underworld, Orpheus is mentioned with respect. And in Plato no other allusion, even to the Orphics, so deprecates the founder of poetry, theology, and civil society, to whom Socrates himself is indebted for more than one happy phrase.[1]

The generally insipid quality of Phaedrus' contribution to the Socratic definition of love in the *Symposium* does not wholly explain why this should be. What for Plato seems to be at issue between Alcestis and Orpheus is the immortality of the soul. For the Homeric thinker who sees immortality as a radical difference between gods and men, the descent into Hades of Orpheus, or Hercules, or Theseus is heroic. For the Platonist who identifies the immortality of the human soul with divinity, it is not. And death becomes, as in the *Alcestis*, less of a finality and more of a religious initiation. But Orpheus, Plato notices, the very founder of rites of initiation, does not give even his earthly life for his beloved.[2]

In Ficino's commentary on the *Symposium* the tone taken towards Orpheus is much less guarded. By this time the Orphica has materialized and been given an honoured place in the Neo-Platonic canon. Orpheus, says Ficino in the opening speech (Giovanni Cavalcanti), best illustrates the universal power of Eros if one regards him as an historical figure, like Alcestis. And in praise of this philosophic lover he makes in the seventh speech (Guido Cavalcanti) one of his several cross-references to the *Phaedrus*.

Orpheus, he explains, was possessed of all four divine madnesses distinguished by Socrates: that of poetry, or the Muses; that of ritual mystery, or Bacchus; that of prophecy, or Apollo; that of love, or Venus. The human soul, being full of discord, needs the music of

---

[1] Cf. *Apology*, 41A; *Ion*, 536B; *Philebus*, 66C; *Laws*, 2.669D, 3.677D, 8.829E.

[2] W. K. C. Guthrie, *The Greeks and Their Gods* (London, 1950), p. 317.

poetry to temper it, the Bacchic sacrifice to unify its parts, the Apolline vision to reveal the transcendent unity behind and before it, and the passion for beauty to unite it with God.[1]

In its concern with psychic unity this gloss resembles the allegory of the judgement of Paris in Ficino's second commentary on the *Philebus*, cited in my Introduction. And the reason why Orpheus rather than Paris should be the titular hero of the first pastoral play begins to appear. Like Socrates in the Dialogues, he is successful in impersonating the desire of rationalist aestheticism for harmony in man, nature, and the divine. Paris, by his preference for Venus, succeeds only in bringing on the Trojan war. (According to Euripides in the *Helen*, he is also cheated by the gods with a mere shadow of his beloved, which disappears.) But Orpheus, both as lover and theologian, is credited with finding a single voice for all the intimations of this world's beauty and the other world's that solicit a human mind.

For Pico, as for other initiates of Ficino's academy, the Orpheus myth is an allegory of the death and new life of the rational soul, lost and found again in the flames of intellectual love. As the lover dies, Pico explains with the cryptic nonchalance of his master, he revives as an angel (*in angelo trasformato*).[2] This metamorphosis will be seen to correspond to the fourth and inward-turning stage of erotic ascent, as described in the *Symposium*, the *Cortegiano*, and many a Renaissance love poem: an ascent in the scale of being from physical desire, as it is called, to desire for union in the soul with the universal first mind where ideal beauty resides.

In such talk the difference between philosophy and poetry disappears. And, whatever advantages an admirer of Donne may find or fail to find in its disappearance, doctrinaire Platonic transcendentalism is responsible. Like the Christianity with which it mingles, Plato's theory of soul, immortality, reincarnation, and the Ideas results in a weakening of Thanatos and a strengthening of Eros. And in the confusion of dying and loving that ensues,

---

[1] *Opera*, ii. 1361–2 (*In Convivium*); cf. i. 927 (*Epistolae*).
[2] Pico, ed. Garin, p. 554 (*Commento*). The whole account of Benivieni's fourth stanza is relevant.

poets of Ficino and Pico's persuasion take an increasingly un-Socratic delight.

From the *Alcestis* to the *Aminta* a less and less tragic language of death makes itself heard:

> I myself, in the transports
> of mystic verses, as in study
> of history and science, have found
> nothing so strong as Compulsion,
> nor any means to combat her,
> not in the Thracian books set down
> in verse by the school of Orpheus
> nor in all the remedies Phoebus has given the heirs
> of Asclepius to fight the many afflictions of man.
>
> (*Alcestis*, ll. 962–71, trans. R. Lattimore.)

The daemon that speaks through Euripides, says Nietzsche, is Socrates. But in the *Aminta*, as in the Daphnis poems and in *Lycidas*, an Orphic voice replaces the Socratic:

> Veramente la legge con che Amore
> Il suo imperio governa eternamente
> Non è dura né obliqua.[1] (*Aminta*, v. i. 1–3)

'For Lycidas your sorrow is not dead.'

In the history of the pastoral play the critical moment of this falling off from a tragic poetry of death into love elegy is—a little absurdly—Poliziano's.

(ii) *Poetry and Mystery*

It is in the *Orfeo* (*c.* 1480) that Platonic theory and Orphic mythology first coincide in a pastoralism that anticipates Tasso's. Guarini, an Aristotelian in criticism, omits all mention of this from the *Compendium*, preferring to acknowledge Beccari's *Sacrificio* (1554) as the prototype. But Poliziano's curious little play remains the classic instance in this mode of the nexus of doctrine and poetry.

For the modern reader there is little to recommend the piece,

---

[1] Truly the law with which Love rules his empire eternally is neither harsh nor devious. Text ed. L. Fassò (Florence, 1943).

either in ethos or style. Its action and language are hardly to be grasped at all, except as allegory. Even Symonds, who by his verse translation pays it a compliment few critics are capable of, calls it improvised and undramatic.[1] What merit it has is best seen in the light of Neo-Platonic theology. This at least enhances it as a curiosity.

The *Orfeo* is a love rite, composed by the Laureate of Ficino's academy, in which the passion of the founder of poetic theology is celebrated. It gives ceremonial expression to the *cultus* of those thinkers and artists who came together under the patronage of Lorenzo de' Medici in the 1470s and 1480s. For most of these Orpheus at some point serves as a topic of the humanistic rhetoric, whether as poetic singer inspired by love, heroic soul searching the limits of nature, or doomed and melancholy sage.

When Ficino in a well-known letter on the Golden Age in Florence refers to 'ancient singing of songs to the Orphic lyre', all three of these figural senses may be understood, the erotic, the hermetic, and the saturnine. Lyric singing is an art which Ficino, like his model Proclus, practised as a part of the religious discipline of *contemplatio*. Traditionally it is a magic practice, but none the less poetic for that, since the power supposedly comes, not from ideas or images, but from the quality of the incantation.[2]

According to Proclus, the efficacy of all such pious imitation of the master is indicated by how fully one is able to conceive of the meaning of his dismemberment, an event which varies markedly in the telling:

Orpheus, on account of his perfect erudition, is reported to have been destroyed in various ways because . . . men of that age participated *partially* of the Orphic harmony: for they were incapable of receiving a universal and perfect science. But the principal part of his melody [i.e., of his mystic doctrine] . . . , the head of Orpheus, is said to have been carried to Lesbos.[3]

[1] J. A. Symonds, *Sketches and Studies in Italy and Greece* (London, 1898), ii. 345–63.
[2] *Opera*, i. 944 (*Epistolae*); *Supplementum Ficinianum*, ii. 87 (ibid.). Cf. Marinus, in *Scriptorum Graecorum Biblioteca* (Paris, 1850), xv. 161–5 (*Vita Procli*); P. Boyancé, *Le Culte des Muses chez les philosophes grecs* (Paris, 1937), p. 163.
[3] Proclus, *In Rempublicam*, i. 174 (ed. W. Kroll), trans. T. Taylor, *Mystical Hymns*

Such a mystique of participation in the Orphic melody would call for as all-inclusive a language of myth as possible, a condition of music; and to this the style of the *Orfeo* constantly aspires.[1] Orpheus means as much to the patron as to the doctors of the Academy. But for Lorenzo in his love poems the contemplation of virtue, whether Orphic or Promethean, takes on a tone of saturnine melancholy:

Active life and contemplative life, inwardness and possession of nature, human love and divine love, all these terms which the wisdom of Ficino would set in hierarchies without breaking the continuity of human endeavour seem to Lorenzo stricken with contradictions which he delights in aggravating. His poetry is the first evidence of those vortices within caused by the influence of the Academy, and shows in some detail the burden of its formulas and myths.[2]

Poliziano at times expresses this troubled and divided mood of the *Selve*, at others the transcendent optimism of the Pico of the *De Hominis Dignitate*. To the Adamo *pichiano*, it is said, the Orfeo *polizianesco* exactly corresponds.[3]

The great virtue of Orpheus for a syncretizing Christian humanist is his having brought the Greek theology out of polytheism into monotheism, and so saved for posterity the fabled wisdom of the gentiles—classical mythology. The heart of his mystery is thus how the many pagan gods are one. This discovery is reputed to have occurred after he visited Egypt and learned the doctrine of Moses (Musaeus).[4] As a victim of dismemberment he personally embodies what syncretic rationalism always assumes, the One in the Many. This includes the Platonic dialectic, defined by Socrates as the god-like art of seeing what can naturally be collected into one and divided into many (*Phaedrus* 266B). So from Moses on that side of

---

of *Orpheus* (London, 1896), pp. l–li. Why Orpheus was destroyed is variously reported as neglect of Bacchus, a grudge borne by Venus concerning Adonis and Persephone, pederasty, misogyny, and despair at the loss of Eurydice.

[1] Cf. Ficino on the soul's striving to 'become everything', i. 310 (*Theologia Platonica*); Pico, *Opera*, p. 106 (*Conclusiones de modo intelligendi hymnos Orphei*).

[2] A. Chastel, *Marsile Ficin et l'art* (Geneva, 1954), pp. 29–30.

[3] E. Garin, in *Il Poliziano e il suo tempo* (Florence, 1957), p. 21; cf. G. Saitta, *Il pensiero italiano nell' umanesimo e nel rinascimento* (Bologna, 1949), i. 545–7.

[4] *Orphicorum Fragmenta*, pp. 255–66 (*ΔΙΑΘΗΚΑΙ*). Tradition differs on whether Orpheus was pupil or teacher.

the New Testament to Proclus on this, there is no theologian, pagan or Christian, whom this shepherd does not prefigure. Orphism, if it ever existed, does not survive—only fragments of its supposed liturgy. What has been recorded of its doctrine— the body as prison of the soul, purgation, vegetarianism—is indistinguishable from Pythagorean psychology.[1] By supplying from aesthetic Platonism the doctrine that is missing, Poliziano rehearses what apparently happened in the Dionysos cult during the Hellenistic and early Christian eras. He makes the Orpheus myth an allegory of the cosmos and the human soul according to Plato.

As myth and as a poetic language, Orphism may be the invention of the early Christian Platonists, or of the Pythagoreans, or of Orpheus himself: it still determines the nature of pastoral in the Renaissance. Orphism and pastoralism are both transmitted by the Platonists. But unlike aesthetic Platonism, Orphism is ascetic; so the mode of poetry that results may be a praise either of pleasure, as in Marlowe, or of puritan virtue, as in Milton, or a reconciliation of the two, as in Marvell.

In its disingenuous simplicity, Poliziano's fable even reflects the two views of classical Orphism at issue in scholarship to this day. Either it is a mystery religion whose god was Dionysos and whose founding priest was Orpheus, or it is a technical term for the ancient myth and ritual that made up the arts of the theatre.[2]

What makes all this implication feasible is the manifold connotation of mythopoeia. It is a trick fundamental to pastoral poetry: bringing to bear in an imitation of Orpheus the power of the hermetic, as well as of Eros and Saturn—a wholesale recourse to that expedient by which a word or image from the rites is given a place in Socratic dialectic.[3]

The point of most poetic treatments of the myth is not that

---

[1] E. R. Dodds, *The Greeks and the Irrational* (Berkeley, 1951), p. 149.

[2] Linforth, pp. 236–42; Guthrie, *Orpheus*, pp. 41–3. Cf. W. Wili, 'Orphic Mysteries and the Greek Spirit' in *The Mysteries* (New York, 1955), pp. 64–92.

[3] Chastel, p. 176; Wind, *Pagan Mysteries*, pp. 14–15. According to Boccaccio, *Genealogia*, v. xii, Hermes (Mercurio) is the donor of the Orphic lyre. Ficino, by his commentary on the Hermetica, encouraged a cult of Mercury corresponding to that of Orpheus; cf. Milton, *Il Penseroso*, l. 88.

Orpheus dies; not in the *Georgics* and *Metamorphoses*, Poliziano's chief sources, not in the *Symposium*, Seneca's tragedies, or the *Consolation of Philosophy*. The point is that the power of Orphic song sways Hades and survives death as a voice in which the Apolline and Bacchic are one. They are always the indivisible brothers, says Ficino; both are exactly the same.[1] So although in the *Orfeo* the death of the hero is represented as the outcome of their rival claims, the mood of this is not tragic at all.

From the prologue announcing a *festa*, spoken by the descending Mercury in some such mediatory pose as Botticelli gives him in the *Primavera*, to the finale of the Bacchantes, who triumphantly return the burden of the play upon the audience—

Ognun segua, Bacco, te[2] (l. 370)—

no hint of tragedy emerges. No lifelike Eurydice gives pathos to her death or to Orfeo's second loss of her. Instead a shadow of the eternal beauty flits before the shepherds who pursue her. No antagonist brings about her death but another of Apollo's shepherd sons, Aristeo. And the death of Orfeo, which is unmarked by any dying speech, suggests not individual defeat but collective victory. This the Bacchantic *kômos* celebrates, more as a remarriage than a death, as in the *Alcestis*.[3]

The plot is as elliptic as a dream. It moves through three phases: *emanatio*, the procession of Mercury and the shepherds; *raptio*, the vision and pursuit of the nymph, first by Aristeo, then by Orfeo; and *remeatio*, the returning procession of Bacchantes. These terms

---

[1] *Opera*, i. 528 (*De Vita*); cf. ii. 1374 (*In Phaedrum*): 'Phoebus enim Baccho proximus corripit, ut etiam mores humanos excedat': For; after Bacchus, Phoebus possesses [man] in such a way that he goes beyond human culture. Cf. Macrobius, *Saturnalia*, I. xviii. 6: 'Euripides in Licymnio Apollinem Liberumque unum eumdemque deum esse significans scribit ... Ad eamdem sententiam Aeschylus': Euripides in his *Licymnius* gives us to understand that Apollo and Liber are one and the same god ... Aeschylus says the same. It is after Boethius that a divergence between Neo-Platonic and Neo-Stoic interpretations of the Orpheus myth, the one pastoral and the other tragic, seems to occur. Cf. D. W. Robertson, Jr., *Preface to Chaucer* (Princeton, 1962), pp. 106–7 n.

[2] Let everyone follow, Bacchus, thee. (Text ed. A. Carducci, rev. A. Donati, Rome, 1910.)

[3] J. A. K. Thomson, *The Greek Tradition* (London, 1915), pp. 111–39.

identify what may be called the pastoral rhythm of action. They are taken from Ficino's account of the movement of Eros through created nature:

The divine beauty in fact creates love in everything; that is, desire for itself. Since God draws the world to himself, and the world is possessed (rapitur), there is a single continuous attraction ... which, as if in a kind of circle, to the place whence it flowed (manavit) returns again (remeat). ... In so far as it begins in God and is proper to him, it is beauty; in so far as it captivates the world in its transit, it is love; in so far as it returns to the Creator and joins its work with him, it is pleasure.[1]

Poliziano expresses the death of Orpheus as just such a gift of Eros to the soul—a euphemism familiar from Platonizing puns on dying (*teleutan*) and being loved by a god (*teletai*), and a late form of the 'failure of nerve'.[2]

If tragedy is absent from the *Orfeo*, pastoralism is present from the first in its most orthodox form. After the prologue of Mercury an eclogue is performed by Aristeo and two other shepherds, the elderly Mopso and the youthful Thyrsis. This and the *cauzona* it gives rise to—

Udite, selve, mie dolci parole[3] (l. 54)—

place the action in an Arcadian landscape and introduce the topic of the inner life.

The procedure here is much the same as in the opening of *Comus*. A descent of the spirit materializes as a bucolic:

... I must put off
These my sky robes spun out of Iris' woof,
And take the weeds and likeness of a swain. (ll. 82–4)

But by comparison the action and language of this part of the *Orfeo* are neither openly Platonic nor, for that matter, puritan.

Poliziano divides his scene among three shepherds who personify the Ages of Man, innocence, folly, and wisdom. When the *coup de*

[1] *Opera*, ii. 1324 (*In Convivium*).
[2] F. M. Cornford, 'Plato and Orpheus', *Classical Review*, xvii (1903), 439; G. Murray, *Five Stages of Greek Religion* (New York, 1955), Ch. IV.
[3] Hear, O woods, my kindly words.

foudre strikes Aristeo in the form of a vision of Euridice, Mopso warns him in Virgilian language that discord will follow:

> Se tu pigli, Aristeo, suo' dure leggi;
> E' t'usciran del capo i sciami et orti
> E viti e biade e paschi e mandrie e gregge.[1] (ll. 41–3)

But love purifies the shepherd's voice, as Aristeo's *canzona* shows. Love-at-first-sight implies Recollection, with its wistful, otherworldly view of the wisdom of innocence. The folly of pastoral passion is the wisdom of erotic Platonism, immanental yet transcendent.

A degenerate form of Socratic *serio ludere* is in action here. While Aristeo sees that Euridice is more lovely than Diana (l. 27), Thyrsis sees that even Venus is not lovelier:

> I' non credo che Vener sia più bella. (l. 103)

This is the usual quasi-*naïveté* of pastoral, an allegorical species of humour. For the shepherds, to whom the mysteries were first revealed, as for the dreamers in Shakespeare, the beauty of Diana and of Venus is that in the end they are one. Such truth may never be revealed except enigmatically and with due ceremony. If it were, there might be doctrine but there would be no poetry.

In the brief second scene the pursuit of the nymph takes place:

> Non mi fuggir, donzella.[2] (l. 125)

This motif informs both remaining configurations of the plot, Orfeo in Hades and Orfeo in search of his own death. It thus makes for an effect of collusion between him and Aristeo. It is against the fate of Orfeo that Aristeo is first warned.

This effect is the greater for Poliziano's avoiding what Tasso later emphasizes, the distinction between shepherd and satyr. Aristeo, like the satyr in the *Aminta*, disappears after bringing on the crisis, leaving it to be resolved by the more complete shepherd, Orfeo. But as little difference of order is implied between the two

---

[1] If you submit, Aristeo, to his cruel laws, you will at once forget your bees and gardens and vines and crops and pastures and flocks and herds.
[2] Fly not from me, maiden.

as between Lycidas and the uncouth swain in Milton. Aristeo's desire for Euridice is proper enough:

> Porgimi, Amor, porgimi or le tue ale![1] (l. 137)

And Orfeo in lamenting her neither blames nor praises him for bringing about her death. The pastoral sense of loss has its antecedent in the tragic, but it rarely amounts to more than what Milton calls 'a pleasing fit of melancholy' (*Comus*, l. 546).

As with Eros and death, so with Logos and passion, an exploitable ambiguity arises, a style which is neither tragic nor comic but a bitter-sweet alternative to either:

> Aristeo ama e disamar non vôle
> Nè guarir cerca di sì dolce doglie:
> Quel loda amor che di lui ben si dole.[2] (ll. 47–9)

This Florentine *dulce amarum* is influenced by the equation of love and death in Ficino and Pico. Poetic mingling of the languages of love and death or pain and pleasure finds its first important Renaissance model in the *Canzoniere* of Petrarch, as does pastoral wordplay on landscape and soul. What Ficino provides is a Platonic-Orphic rationale:

Love is called by Plato bitter, and not unjustly, because death is inseparable from love. And Orpheus called love γλυκύπικρον [bitter-sweet] . . . because love is a voluntary death.[3]

In the history of literature poetry usually precedes doctrine, just as allegory gives place to the genre piece. It is therefore to the credit of aesthetic Platonism in Florence that it gives rise to a style of poetry still sometimes called pure. The humanist theory of allegory has a part in this process, and a more sophisticated one than might be supposed. For it does not encourage the mere translation of concepts into the language of art, or vice versa. It calls for a style which as a mode of perception goes beyond what Blake calls 'corporeal understanding'.

It is a ridiculous demand which England and America make, writes an American pastoralist of the nineteenth century, 'that

---

[1] Give me, O Love, give me thy wings.

[2] Aristeo loves and would not love not or seek to cure so sweet a pain: he praises love who suffers from it well.

[3] *Opera*, ii. 1327 (*In Convivium*); Wind, *Pagan Mysteries*, p. 135.

you shall speak so that they can understand you'.[1] And this I take to be the point of Yeats's stricture upon the language of aesthetic Platonism in Spenser—that it asks to be translated into concepts:

Allegory and, to a much greater degree, symbolism . . . can speak of things which cannot be spoken of in any other language, but one will always, I think, feel some sense of unreality when they are used to describe things which can be described as well in ordinary words.[2]

The usage of 'unreality' here is worthy of Ficino or Poliziano. Whatever their vices, neither thought that allegory—the awakening of the soul from the sleep of human life—was any less than a sheer poetic style.

The difficulty with the *Orfeo* is that neither the ear nor the hand of the best lyric poet between Lorenzo and Michelangelo is evident in it. It is a collocation of octaves, *canzonette*, *ballate*, and Latin metres that like so much mythological poetry lacks an intelligible tone. What may explain this is the coming home to roost in pastoral of Socratic-Orphic poetics.

There are some notorious reflections on the style proper to philosophers and theologians in a letter of Pico's dated 1485. Melanchthon later refers to it as 'vituperative of anything eloquent'. Ostensibly, Pico defends the barbarous prose of the Scholastics by arguing that philosophy and rhetoric are incompatible. But Melanchthon seems to have overlooked the element of play in this argument. In actual performance it amounts to a theory and practice of the oracular, modelled on Socrates under his satyric aspect:

One reads the sacred stories, written rustically rather than elegantly, for precisely the reason that in . . . true knowing nothing is more . . . detrimental than . . . elaborated . . . discourse. The latter belongs. . . in forums, not to questions about natural and celestial things . . . in the academy. . . . We [philosophers] are not unlike the ancients who by their riddles and by the masks of their fables made uninitiates shun the mysteries; and we have been wont . . . to drive them from our feasts. . . . Yet I shall indicate the form of our discourse. It is the same

[1] H. D. Thoreau, *Walden* (Boston, 1906), p. 356. Thoreau's is a unique, self-made variation on the Orphic voice. In America pastoralism remains allegory but this is compromised by the notion that Arcadia has at last been located.

[2] W. B. Yeats, *The Cutting of an Agate* (London, 1919), p. 200.

as that of the Sileni of our Alcibiades [*Symposium*, 215–17]. . . . But, you will say, modern ears do not tolerate here irregular, there disconnected, and always unharmonious constructions. . . . Adopt those ears of Tyaneus by which . . . he would hear not earthly Marsyas but celestial Apollo compose on a divine cither a cosmic melody in ineffable modes.[1] (*Opera*, pp. 351–8, trans. Q. Breen)

The prose style in question has been well defined as prophetic: 'the truth . . . of it we are to accept without proof. . . . Brevity and disjointedness are therefore no accident.'[2]

Pico mentions Poliziano as privy to this correspondence, and the brevity and disjointedness of the *Orfeo* suggest that, as a poetic theologian, its author shares the philosopher's distrust of words as the vehicle of wisdom. Poliziano writes rustically rather than elegantly on principle. One may be no more satisfied by this 'studied barbarity' than Johnson is by Spenser's in the *Shepheardes Calender*:

Surely, at the same time that a shepherd learns theology he may gain some acquaintance with his native language. (*The Rambler*, No. 37)

But a fundamental premiss of pastoral style is still to be recognized. Its musicality is by design harsh. The mask of the fable is meant to drive all but the initiated from the feast.

To be initiated is to be made self-aware. And De Sanctis, who in his own way writes well about the *Orfeo*, assumes an unusual self-awareness in the audience at Mantua for whom it was commissioned:

Just as the burghers, dressed up as knights, reproduced the world of chivalry, these new Athenians . . . must have thoroughly enjoyed watching each other parade. . . . There was enormous enthusiasm when Baccio Ugolini, dressed as Orfeo and holding a zither in his hand, came down the mountain singing the praises of the Cardinal in magnificent Latin verses. . . . We must think of the actors and the decorations and the songs and the music, and the excitement of a

---

[1] Q. Breen, 'G. Pico della Mirandola on the Conflict of Philosophy and Rhetoric', *Journal of the History of Ideas*, xiii (1952), 396–8. Cf. Petrarca, *Familiari*, x. 4; Boccaccio, *Genealogia*, XIV. xii: 'quod inextricabile est, artificiosius videatur esse compositum': [the purpose of the poet is] to make what is incomprehensible appear to be wrought with exquisite artistry (trans. C. Osgood).

[2] H. Brown, *Prose Styles* (Minneapolis, 1966), p. 71.

society that saw it as a living reflection of itself. . . . There is nothing serious in this world except what is given it by the imagination.[1]

All that he overlooks is the profuse, if quaint, learning for which this playful aestheticism is a veil. The makers of Renaissance pastoral, poets and audiences, are esoterics. And to write on their plan it is at least necessary to read Plato and think like Ficino and Pico.[2]

All poetry is traditionally said to have arisen from the practice of veiling sacred truth from the profane. Petrarch and Boccaccio are the modern authorities for this. As a matter of poetics as well as doctrine, an Orpheus poem should be hermetic. And with the hermetic, as with the Socratic, what begins as verbal play is expected to persist as myth and dream.

With the scene of his playing the lyre, Orfeo enters upon a ministry which reveals him as Apolline prophet and Bacchic man of sorrows. It is between these two gods that he must be torn, yet he of all heroes best knows that they are one. The handling of this mystery speaks for some hermetic skill on Poliziano's part:

> Oimè, che 'l troppo amore
> N'ha disfatti ambe dua.[3] (ll. 306–7)

He makes the famous condition of not looking back the crisis of the shepherd's life, dividing him between Apollo and his indivisible brother whom the Orphics call the son of Persephone. Here, if anywhere, he achieves as a playwright the hierophantic manner of the Orphic philosopher, an 'elliptical vulgarization which enabled him to hint at the secrets he professed to withhold'.[4] Yet little of this delightful mystification is to be felt in the words themselves—much less than in Tasso or Milton.

With a contemporary the naturalizing of the myth in the *quattrocento* court would no doubt count for much. But could it count for more than the accumulated lore of which any such humanist

---

[1] F. De Sanctis, *Storia della letteratura italiana* (Bari, 1925), i. 346 (trans. J. Redfern).

[2] Cf. Chastel, p. 144, for Poliziano as accredited purveyor of enigmas and emblems to the Florentine circle. Macrobius, *Somnium Scipionis*, I. ii. 9, also regards the Orpheus fable as a Pythagorean mystery.

[3] Alas, too great a love has undone us both.

[4] Wind, *Pagan Mysteries*, p. 19.

compliment is made? As nowadays with Cocteau's Orpheus film, the more one knows of how the myth has been interpreted the more one is likely to be pleased. Even the pederastic second elegy, which for Poliziano has its exoteric side, recalls the ethos of the Dialogues and the survival of the singing head in Lesbos. But this is still not to say that the *Orfeo* has much more to recommend it than erudition, scandal, and parade.

Part of the disappointment of reading this play is that the Orphic voice is not rendered in the person of the hero. He sings each phase of his metamorphosis except the last and most important one, the one in which the Apolline is shown to have its satyric side. This the Bacchantes sing. It is as if there were no last speech in Marlowe's tragedy of Orphic aspiration, only a chorus of the devils who dismember Faustus.

Yet the same disappointment faces a reader of Virgil, since the only utterance of the immortal Orpheus in the *Georgics* is the name Eurydice, a helpless word upon the lips.[1] And where in Milton's Ludlow masque is the final all-embracing voice of temperance, answering and comprehending the satyric magnificence of Comus? There are only those limpid songs. The understanding seems to be that the mystery—the divine comedy—of collective individuation can only be implied, the actuality of it only assumed. This understanding the pastoralist shares with the Platonist: 'He that would speak exactly must not name [the One].'[2]

In this event the Arcadian *personae* cannot, as Guarini thinks, make the pastoral. On the contrary, the fable is the thing, not the shepherd figure. The poet, himself, in his own person everywhere in the poem, has the only voice that is Orphic. This supposes a peculiar self-awareness which has its academic rationale: a continuous line of inspired singers coming from earliest times and including Adam and David no less than Ovid and Poliziano.

Pastoral poetry is thus not so much dramatic as eponymous.

[1] Virgil, *Georgics*, iv. 523-7; M. Bodkin, *Archetypal Patterns in Poetry* (London, 1934), p. 202.
[2] Cf. Plotinus, *Enneads*, VI. ix. 3 (trans. E. R. Dodds, *Select Passages Illustrating Neoplatonism*).

And to its priestly succession the Renaissance poet or critic often alludes by its eponym, as witness Milton in the *Allegro*.[1] Something of the same sense enters into that identifying of the poet by his pastoral alias, familiar in the case of Astrophil, or Colin Clout, or the Shepherd of the Ocean.

Accordingly what Poliziano brings to a close in the Chorus of Bacchantes is a serial, not an actual, rendering of the Orphic voice. In this scene his whole mode of composition may be observed, the one meaning towards which the several ellipses of his plot and language move. Love myth and allegory of the soul are transposed to conscious art; a rite by which the play is made the subject of itself.

The audience, gathered into the action at the entry of Orfeo praising the house of Gonzaga, is now called on to consummate the ceremony by drinking the blood of Bacchic sacrifice:

> Ognun gridi Bacco Bacco,
> E pur cacci del vin giù
> Poi con suoni farem fiacco.
> Bevi tu, e tu, e tu.[2] (ll. 393–6)

There is only the faintest reflex of the maenadism of the *Bacchae* to be felt in this exhortation.

> The riot of the tipsy Bacchanals,
> Tearing the Thracian singer in their rage,

draws the audience's attention to itself as an audience, and so returns it laughingly upon its own reality, of which the *festa* has been, as Johnson would say, only a reminder. It is thus the 'magic potency of the theater' that Poliziano finally invokes; the mystery of which the 'arts of Dionysos and Orpheus' are the rite.[3]

---

[1] ll. 135–50; cf. Ficino, i. 927 (*Epistolae*): 'In collibus Ambre Agnanaeque vallens [*sic*] Laurens ille Phoebeus Dionysio nectare passim ebrius debacchatur': In the hills and vale of Ambra and Agnana (?) Lorenzo, that Apolline poet, rages everywhere, drunk with the nectar of Dionysos: or, in present-day academese: Lorenzo's idyllic manner is a complex fusion of the ratiocinative with the passionate and rhapsodic. Cf. E. Spenser, *Shepheardes Calender*, October: 'For Bacchus fruit is frend to Phoebus wise' (l. 106), where the context is again Orphic and Socratic.

[2] Everyone cry 'Bacchus, Bacchus', and drink down the wine, then with sounds [of flute and cymbal] we'll dance until we drop. Drink, you, and you, and you.

[3] F. Fergusson, *The Idea of a Theater* (Princeton, 1949), pp. 123–4; Linforth,

Renaissance pastoralism here takes on its theatrical form. The audience is given a familiar classical fable adapted to the Christian form of *sacra rappresentazione*. Since the founder of poetic theology is involved, it is also being given a pagan love mystery. A lover-poet suffers a pseudo-martyrdom. A courtly patron is congratulated. Apollo is honoured and the air fills with a singing to the lyre. Bacchus is propitiated and the earth moves to the dithyramb. The Orphic voice encloses all. Art is, nature is, culture is. It is Proteus who in the *Georgics* tells this fable to make the bees of Aristaeus swarm. In the *Orfeo* the mystery is the same: the One found among the Many in the name of the Panic saviour of every shepherd's Protean soul.

In the myth of Orpheus, says Symonds, 'the humanism of the Revival became conscious of itself'.[1] This is well said. Throughout the sixteenth century the dominant mode of poetic and dramatic consciousness remains mythological, though the search for a style proper to the erotic whole man goes well beyond the limits of pastoral, as witness Marlowe's *Faustus*. But even within these limits Poliziano's version of the myth is deficient. His Orphic voice, like the voice of Socrates, is homoerotic—in spite of Euridice, in spite of Diotima. In Giorgione's *Concert champêtre* it is at each other that the shepherds still gaze. But between the *Phaedrus* and the *Orfeo* the most significant event for pastoralism is the making of the myth of courtly love. Of this Tasso's Orphic voice takes account.

p. 237: ‘τὸ φιλότεχνον τὸ περὶ τὰς Διονυσιακὰς τέχνας καὶ τὰς Ὀρφικάς᾽ (Strabo, *Geography*, X. iii. 23).

[1] *Renaissance in Italy*, IV. i. 358. Cf. E. Sewell, *The Orphic Voice* (New Haven, 1960), p. 47.

2

THE SHEPHERD'S LIFE

Pastoral, n.s. A poem in which any action or passion is
represented by its effects upon a country life.

JOHNSON

(i) *Love and Landscape*

THE *Aminta* (1573–90) has all the features of orthodox pastoral—
an Arcadian landscape, shepherds, a satyr, nymphs, a celebration
of the Golden Age. But these are ordered in a way one has not
always been led to expect.

Tasso's pastoralism is a psychology of the love passion. All the
classic symptoms of tragic love are present under a serio-comic
aspect; the love of love, the love of death, the indifference to social
and Christian sanction, the sense of a mystical initiation, the wilful
mutual suffering:

> Non so se il molto amaro
> Che provato ha costui servendo, amando,
> Piangendo e disperando,
> Raddolcito esser puote pienamente
> D'alcun dolce presente.[1] (v. i. 140–4)

'Nell'*Aminta*', says Croce, 'domina l'amore passione.'[2]

The plot itself could not be simpler:

> The chaste nymph . . . is won over by the fervent will to martyrdom
> and the would-be suicide of the amorous shepherd. That is all.[3]

---

[1] I do not know if the great bitterness he has suffered, serving, loving, weeping,
despairing, can be wholly sweetened by any present joy.

[2] B. Croce, *Poeti e scrittori del pieno e del tardo rinascimento* (Bari, 1945–53), i. 336:
In the *Aminta* the love passion predominates.

[3] K. Vossler, 'Tassos Aminta und die Hirtendichtung', *Studien zur vergleichenden
Literaturgeschichte*, vi (1906), 37.

But as the cant terms of this summary suggest, the conflict is as much between Aminta and Silvia and the other shepherds as between the lovers themselves:

> These are two violent, self-willed young people, blindly true to their notions of themselves, who reject with all the impetus of youth the counsels of their more experienced confidants.[1]

And it is part of the sense of this action that they never confront one another on stage. Their private flirtations with love and death take place only in a series of dialogues with confidants or with the chorus, where their absurdity is least distracting.

It is possible for Shakespearians to underrate this convention of an alien theatre. As the five acts unfold the passion of Aminta is continually upstaged, as it were, and given anterior or mythic standing. Between it and the audience which sees it with the mind's eye only there falls the entire plot, a vocal interplay of attitudes towards love. This, and not the fable itself, is the mirror held up to nature. In it the courtly audience sees an image of itself under the species of the inner life.

The Platonism of this device is unmistakable, and so is the pastoralism. Aminta and Silvia act out a mutual passion but are in fact in love with the idea of loving, Love itself. In the words and gestures of the poet's finding there is enacted only one version of Love. And for the rationalist purposes of such a fiction stock Arcadian *personae* have a certain advantage:

> The use of 'constant characters' . . . guarantees exactitude and . . . even . . . veracity to the interplay of emotion. Here it is art and not 'life' that directs matters. We are in the presence of a creation of the mind, and not of a confusion of cloudy reflections, of more or less damaging admissions, and undeserved bits of luck (as novels are today).[2]

De Rougemont writes here of the *Astrée*, but the same may be said of the *Aminta*. What vitiates life in the present is that it must be lived before it can be remembered. Not so in the art of pastoral.

---

[1] M. Gerhardt, *La Pastorale* (Assen, 1950), pp. 111.
[2] De Rougemont, p. 185 (trans. M. Belgion).

The shepherd's life is the inner life. It is on this equation that the virtues of pastoral in a Platonizing age are founded. What should we think of the shepherd's life, says Thoreau, if his sheep always pastured higher than his thoughts? And Tasso is by inclination a poet of the inner life, a fact nowhere more evident than in his poem of heroic action, the *Gerusalemme liberata*. His poetic gift is eminently suited to the subject of the love passion, which always asks to be acknowledged as a private state or crisis of mind.

The *Aminta* thus differs markedly from a non-pastoral, such as the *Mandragola*. For all its concern with the courtship of lovers, one of whom is feverish and the other coldly chaste, Machiavelli's is a play about society, not passion—the politics of sex—'un gioco di forze'.[1] It stands in the extrovert, cynical line of Terence and Plautus, while Tasso's play is introvert and idyllic, looking back to Virgil for its model of shepherdly love:

> . . . tamquam haec sit nostri medicina furoris,
> aut deus ille malis hominum mitescere discat.[2]
> *(Bucolics,* x. 60–1)

It also looks forward to the *Nouvelle Héloise* and *Lady Chatterley's Lover*, two more landscapes of the mind.

In pastoral the means to an effect of the lover's inner world is landscape. Like Plato in the *Phaedrus*, Tasso begins with places and trees, a retreat into the woods and the dwellings of the humble:

> Ricovero ne' boschi e ne le case
> De le genti minute. (Prologue, ll. 31–2)

Thus Amore, the Eros *fuggitivo*, who speaks the prologue in the mortal part of a shepherd (*sotto pastorali spoglie*). The paradox, in poetry as in painting, is that landscape leads into rather than out of the self-conscious mind.

Not all landscapes give this effect. The Limbourg brothers' *Juillet*, for all its bucolic detail and colours of passion, lacks the full inwardness of Italianate pastoral. It stands, says an authority,

---

[1] De Sanctis, ii. 91.
[2] As if this [anything I do in the woods] would cure my madness or the god learn pity for man's suffering.

'halfway between symbol and fact'.[1] But in the landscapes one would light on as having most in common with Tasso's—the *Concert Champêtre*, the *Sacred and Profane Love*—Giorgione and Titian are clearly allegorists intent on 'interiorization'. Their scenery is less lifelike than lovelike, as Rossetti says of Beatrice. The formulary language by which Tasso locates the *Aminta* similarly evokes less a place than a frame of mind. He addresses his audience directly in the prologue but speaks in parables. Arcadia is not specified, only 'these woods', 'Diana's train', 'this mountain nymph', 'a crowd of shepherds garlanded and holding festival', the 'rustic pipe'. And the flora and fauna of the region, it turns out —beeches, palms, bees, thorns, wolves, and sheep—have their sanction, not in natural history, but in the art culture of an audience for whom such symbols are meaningful.

This is not a culture confined to Italian court circles, any more than pastoral is necessarily exclusive of naturalistic detail. Pastoral landscape is always to be understood emblematically, in the light of a tradition of art—even by the public for whom the forest of Arden, with its palms and olives and lions, was invented. There are bears in Shakespeare's Bohemia, just as in Ovid's Arcadia.[2]

Life in such a landscape is conceived of, says Pater, 'as a sort of listening'. If one inquires what the shepherd listens for, the answer presumably is Platonic—'a kind of music in the very nature of things'.[3] The frame of mind evoked is thus aesthetic. And the shepherd in search of cosmic beauty expects, like Socrates, to listen to himself:

non canimus surdis; respondent omnia silvae.[4] (*Bucolics*, x. 8)

This proves to be the case in the *duecento* pastourelle and the Petrarchan idyll of solitude, as well as the Virgilian eclogue:

[1] K. Clark, *Landscape into Art* (London, 1949), p. 12.
[2] Cf. Curtius, pp. 190–5.
[3] W. Pater, *The Renaissance* (London, 1910), p. 151; *Plato and Platonism* (London, 1910), p. 268. Cf. E. H. Gombrich, 'Renaissance Artistic Theory and the Development of Landscape Painting', *Gazette des beaux-arts*, xli (1953), 344; Cassirer, *Individuum und Kosmos*, p. 151: 'So wird für Petrarca die Landschaft zum lebendigen Spiegel des Ich': So for Petrarch landscape becomes the living mirror of the Self.
[4] We do not sing unheard; to every word the woods respond.

In un boschetto trova' pasturella. . . .[1]

(Guido Cavalcanti, *Rime*, xlvi, ed. G. Favati)

Solo e pensoso i più deserti campi. . . .[2]

(Petrarch, *Canzoniere*, xxxv)

. . . tamen cantabitis, Arcades, inquit
montibus haec vestris: soli cantare periti. . . .[3]

(*Bucolics*, x. 31–2)

. . . las canziones que sólo el monte oía. . . .[4]

(Garcilaso, *Églogas*, i. 423)

Though the number and gender of the shepherd voices may vary,
the reflexive function of landscape remains constant.
In the *Aminta* accordingly, it is to the woods that the reason of
love is argued:

> Queste selve oggi ragionar d'Amore
> Udranno in nuova guisa: e ben parassi
> Che la mia deità sia qui presente
> In sé medesma e non ne' suoi ministri.[5]
>
> (Prol. ll. 76–9)

And Aminta himself confirms this practice. First he makes it sound
Orphic:

> Ho visto a 'l pianto mio
> Risponder per pietate i sassi e l'onde,
> E sospirar le fronde.[6] (I. ii. 246–8)

Then Socratic:

> Io son contento,
> Tirsi, a te dir ciò che le selve e i monti

---

[1] In a little wood I found a shepherdess.
[2] Alone and full of thought, the more deserted fields [I pace].
[3] . . . Yet will you sing, Arcadians, this tale to the mountains: you alone know how
to sing.
[4] . . . Songs which only the mountain hears.
[5] Today these woods shall hear the argument of love in a new form: and my
godhead shall appear in his own person and not that of his ministers. (Cf. *Ion*,
534D.)
[6] I have seen rocks and waves in pity answer my complaint, and the leaves sigh.

E i fiumi sanno, e gli uomini non sanno:
Ch'io sono omai sì presso a la mia morte.[1]
(I. ii. 288–91)

This use of landscape as a sounding-board has its counterpart in the
opening scene between nymph and shepherdess. The complaisant
Dafne argues her case for love by the same analogy from nature:

Amano ancora
Gli arbori. Veder puoi con quanto affetto
E con quanti iterati abbracciamenti
La vite s'avviticchia a 'l suo marito.[2] (I. i. 150–3)

Tongues in trees, sermons in stones, as Shakespeare's Duke says of
Arden, and 'good in everything'. He adds, 'I would not change it.'
(*AYLI*, II. i. 16–18.)
    What does landscape mean in the *Aminta*? As much, no doubt, as
one's imagination allows. And what may a language of myth not
imply? But to begin with, it means the mind of love, erotic, impassioned, and viewed from within. Life in the woods means the
acting out of certain inner states which for the Renaissance find
their classic symbol in shepherdliness. These, however, are conceivable only as the mental states of courtly or urbane persons.
    The distinction between city-court and countryside so much
emphasized by students of pastoralism is thus for Tasso—as for
Theocritus, Virgil, and Shakespeare—largely an allegory. It is
understood that an actual ecology informs any imitation of simple,
natural, rural life; observation will in some way inform every invention. But the use of landscape with figures in pastoral is best
understood as a conscious fiction. It comes of the readiness of refined
poets and their audiences to accept a life very different from their
own as symbolic. What it symbolizes is a virtuous inwardness which
Plato and the Bible both prefer to any worldly life that courtiers or
country people actually live.

_____

[1] I am content, Tirsi, to tell you what the woods and hills and rivers know, and
men do not know: that I am now so close to my death.
[2] Even the trees are in love. You can see how dearly and how often the vine
entwines herself with the one to whom she is wedded.

(ii) *Courtier, Satyr, and Nymph*

If the place of the shepherd figure in poetry is warranted it should have more to recommend it than a familiar emblematic meaning. Poetic symbolism usually combines two modes of expression, one traditional, the other novel. Imagination operates by 'fusing old ideas in such a way as to generate new ones', as well as by 'grasping the . . . transient image in relation to something more universal and perduring'. The former is the metaphoric way.[1] What claim to the novelty of metaphor can be made for a symbol as old as Orpheus or Moses?

It is curious how little overt association Tasso's shepherds have with Hebraic Christianity. They have none. As emblems, their explicit connection is all with Athens, Rome, Alexandria. No doubt biblical associations obtain—with the *Song of Solomon* especially— but not in the words as words. What evidently does obtain, from the opening direction 'Amore in abito pastorale' onwards, is an implication of quite another sort. Aminta is not only the Orphic lover-poet under the aspect of the inner life, he is also the *cinquecento* courtier:

> Si canimus silvas, silvae sint consule dignae.[2]
>
> (*Bucolics*, iv. 3)

In this resounding line there is an ambiguity as modish for Tasso and his audience as for Virgil and his. A myth is 'not a fiction imposed on one's already given world, but a way of apprehending that world'.[3]

That scholars should rather have emphasized the emblematic meaning of the shepherd is no surprise. Yet a preference for doctrine over poetry might equally have led to an understanding of this symbol as a metaphor, its tenor supplied from the *trattati d'amore*. For the *Aminta* is a poet's vision of the same theory that is given its most familiar doctrinal form by Castiglione in the *Cortegiano*: the perfecting of the courtier's life through love.

---

[1] Wheelwright, p. 123.
[2] If our song is of the woods, let the woods be worthy of a consul.
[3] Wheelwright, p. 159.

Both the *Aminta* and the *Cortegiano* are underwritten by the Platonic aestheticism of Ficino and his school. Tasso, by a use of landscape and shepherd figures, limits himself to the courtier's contemplative life, the service of the lady as nymph, while Castiglione discusses the active life as well, the service of the prince in politics and war. But he devotes his third book to the *cortegiana*, and in the fourth, after the entry of the Magnifico Giuliano de' Medici (Alcibiades), he concludes with a pseudo-Socratic oration on love. Reconciling these two ways of life, however, though mandatory for the courtly apologist in the Renaissance, is not within Castiglione's powers of dialectic. This must be what makes Burckhardt say that the famous concluding speech given to Bembo is extrinsic to the whole.[1]

As in the *Aminta*, a studied manner and style are made to count for everything. Even the ascent of the soul to intellectual contemplation of divine beauty is a conscious process of alienation. It involves retreat, the erotic abandonment of sense and reason, followed by an inscaping of the mind. Hence the praise of that seed of courtly folly in everyone (*nascosa virtù di pazzia*) which, says Cesare Gonzaga, can come to unlimited fruition:

Thus, one turned out to be foolish in verse, another in music, another in love . . . another in riding, another in fencing. . . .

(I. viii, trans. C. Singleton)

Such folly is Erasmian; and the fruit of it in the courtier is a graceful nonchalance in all things (*sprezzatura*), a virtue which the shepherd in his silliness towards the world personifies. 'Passione pronta allo sbaraglio' is Croce's apt phrase for it.[2]

The mark of the courtly, as of the pastoral, is thus play, humour, wit, exercised as a principle rather than on occasion. Man, says Bibbiena, 'is a risible animal . . . what we laugh at is nearly always something incongruous, and yet not amiss' (II. xlv–xlvi). The *Cortegiano* is itself a species of the comic, as is the *Aminta*. Hence, the *serio ludere* of their mutual definition of love.

An old courtier, argues Bembo, can be a better lover than a young

---

[1] Burckhardt, iii. 262.
[2] Croce, i. 336: Passion apt for disorder.

one, love being a desire to enjoy beauty through perception of the highest order attainable (IV. ii). And the paradox is as much Orphic as Socratic in that it makes courtly love a lifelong calling like the shepherd's. For every youthful Orfeo or Aminta there is usually an elderly Mopso or Elpino.

In the young, sensual or satyric love is excusable, but a rational or shepherdly passion is happier, since beauty is properly the object of vision and hearing, not the other senses. In rational love the kiss may be granted, as in the *Song of Solomon*. This is finally granted to Aminta (V. i. 105), but the happiest love, according to Bembo, is intellectual, or divine. Accordingly it is nothing less than apotheosis that Aminta undergoes by his erotic martyrdom and rebirth in the flames of passion.

The grace that perhaps saves all this talk in Castiglione is the unfanatic nonchalance of his style. It depends how much credit one is ready to grant a mere manner in literature. Certainly the refinement sought after is less feasible in courtesy-book prose than in Tasso's mythological poetry.

The satyr, like Morello in Castiglione's dialogue, is the courtier under a partial aspect of his inner life—the Bacchic. He is the shepherd *manqué*, unpurged, irrepressibly natural. And as nature anticipates art, so the satyr has in him the makings of the courtier as Orphic shepherd. Whoever is not attracted to Nature and Proteus will approach Pan in vain.

Making this point is something of a sophistry, because it is one which no one denies. But few wish to approve of it either. Carrara, for example, prefers to complain that in the elegy on love Tasso's satyr sounds incongruously like a courtier.[1] So he does:

> Picciola è l'ape, e fa co'l picciol morso
> Pur gravi e pur moleste ferite:
> Ma qual cosa è più picciola d'Amore?[2] (II. i. 1–3)

The result is proper to the whole mode of shepherdly and satyric masking in which the *Aminta* is written. And the play of connota-

[1] E. Carrara, *La poesia pastorale* (Milan, 1909), p. 338.
[2] The bee is small, and with a small sting makes wounds that are severe and full of pain. But what thing is it that is smaller than Love?

tion here, cultivated against licentious, is a wit that in English comes to its maturity in the school of Donne. To see its early promise in Tasso one must forget about decorum except as *discordia concors*, a certain incongruity immanent in all mythological thinking. As always in pastoral, the model for this is Socratic-Orphic, the Dialogues rediscovered as a bible full of mysteries:

That Socrates, who was a disciple of Apollo . . . should be figuratively described by the drunken Alcibiades as a Silenus or Marsyas, meant that his ruthless pursuit of bewildering questions was but the disguise of an inward clarity—a disguise which was indispensable because it reckoned with the twofold nature of man. To bring out the hidden clarity in others, whose souls were covered and confused by their bodies, required a cathartic method, a Dionysian ordeal by which the 'terrestrial Marsyas' is tortured so that the 'heavenly Apollo' may be crowned.[1]

In the Neo-Platonic language of pastoral myth, the Apolline flaying of Marsyas and the Bacchic tearing of Orpheus paraphrase the same mystical proposition: that the way to self-knowledge is through loss of self.

Not every Renaissance Italian satyr scene is courtly, as witness Piero's allegory of culture, the *Discovery of Honey*. But the readiness of a sixteenth-century court to see itself under the species of the satyric is evident in the *Feast of the Gods*, Bellini's quaint mythological portrait of the Ferrarese circle, *c.* 1514. Here is Cardinal Bembo as Silenus, complete with ass, the infant Ercole d'Este as Bacchus, Bellini himself as Silvanus, and an unidentified courtier as Priapus, honouring the union of Alfonso I and Lucrezia Borgia with a satyric tableau. As in the *Fasti*, Priapus is about to ravish Vesta when the ass of Silenus brays and she awakes and flees. Presiding is Cardinal Ippolito d'Este in the guise of Mercury.[2]

In the *Aminta* as in the *Orfeo*, it is the satyr who brings on the crisis of the shepherd's life:

---

[1] Wind, *Pagan Mysteries*, p. 143.
[2] E. Wind, *Bellini's Feast of the Gods* (Cambridge, Mass.), 1948, pp. 36–44.

> Io, perché non per mia salute adopro
> La vïolenza, se mi fe' natura
> Atto a far vïolenze ed a rapire?[1] (II. i. 78–80)

In an absurd scene, saved from banality by *oratio obliqua*, the satyr takes flight after tying Silvia to a tree, and Aminta is left to look on Silvia's beauty in the naked flesh:

> Come la fuga de l'altro concesse
> Spazio a lui di mirare, egli rivolse
> I cupidi occhi in quelle membra belle,
> Che, come suole tremolare il latte
> Ne' giunchi, sì parean morbide e bianche;
> E tutto 'l vidi sfavillar ne 'l viso.[2] (III. i. 72–7)

Scenes like this pose as awkward a question as could be asked on how pastoral may be understood. Greg takes it to be merely licentious, 'fiddling harmonics on the strings of sensualism'.[3] And if Tasso were not the contemporary and rival of Titian one might agree. The least to be said is that there are more ways than one of looking at Counter-Reformation mythologies.

The tone of the *Aminta* is mystical as well as sensual, and as a clue to this the *Sacred and Profane Love* serves where healthy common sense will not. Of Titian's two female figures at the fountain of Amore, the *donna ignuda* symbolizes for Platonism the higher and celestial desire.[4] Behind her lies the customary ideal landscape, allegorical and with pastoral lovers. And at this stage of erotic ascent, as in the *Aminta*, there is no longer a satyr in view.

The pastoral is as much a man's world as the heroic. Nymph and shepherdess are not personalities but images of woman. In this they conform to that transparency by means of which pastoral could so readily become opera. As one listens to the arias of Silvia or Dafne it is clear that Tasso writes, not a comedy of manners, but a

---

[1] Why do I not for my wellbeing resort to force, if Nature has made me apt for forcing and carrying off?

[2] When the other's flight gave him space to wonder, he turned his longing gaze upon those beauteous limbs which trembled white as spume among the rushes, and I saw his face all aglow.

[3] W. W. Greg, *Pastoral Poetry and Pastoral Drama* (London, 1906), p. 192.

[4] Wind, *Pagan Mysteries*, p. 122.

Romance of the Rose adapted to the stage.[1] Like shepherd and satyr, these are figures in a play of shadows and represent a lover's inner life collectively. But for a lustre or so, all are of the same mind concerning beauty, chastity, and pleasure:

> Perduto è tutto il tempo
> Che in amar non si spende.[2] (I. i. 30–1)

The question is, as for Shakespeare, what is love? When Dafne tries to waken in the prudish Silvia her own urgent desire for pleasure:

> Cangia, cangia consiglio,
> Pazzarella che sei[3] (I. i. 38–9)

this is as much a matter of her being on the side of nature as being naughty and cynical.[4] The scene itself calls for something other than literal interpretation—as do the images of dream and fantasy in actual experience. It is by bringing them to consciousness and understanding them that morals may be served. Tasso's means of doing so are mythological and Platonic: the figures of Chastity and Pleasure composed on the principle of *discordia concors* or, as Pico defines it, Beauty.[5]

The *Primavera* helps illuminate this crucial pastoral device. In Botticelli's triad of Graces, Chastity and Pleasure are brought face to face in a ritual dance by Beauty, under the aim of Cupid's fiery shaft. Tasso's Silvia also is, according to Amore, the cruellest nymph that ever followed in Diana's train:

> Io voglio oggi con questo
> Far cupa e immedicabile ferita
> Nel duro sen de la più cruda ninfa
> Che mai seguisse il coro di Dïana.[6] (Prol. ll. 52–5)

---

[1] Cf. Olschki, *Poesia del Cinquecento*, pp. 42–5. For the pastoral origins of opera, cf. J. Kerman, *Opera as Drama* (London, 1957), pp. 25–49.

[2] The time is all lost that is not spent in love.

[3] Change, change, I counsel you, foolish little one.

[4] Greg, p. 191.

[5] Pico, ed. Garin, p. 495: 'la discordia concorde, il che si può per vera deffinizione assignare di essa bellezza' (*Commento*). Cf. Ficino, II. 1324 (*In Convivium*).

[6] Do both the arrow [*questo dardo*] and the torch [*face*] turn into the thyrsis

Today he has laid aside his wings, quiver, and bow, yet with torch changed to shepherd's staff he will still inflict in her cold breast the secret mortal wound of flames unseen (ll. 45–52). All her delight, Silvia now protests, is the care of bow and arrows (I. i. 12).

To grasp the mode of an art like this, the very last help one needs is the present-day ability to identify with the dramatis personae. Dafne mentions in passing that Silvia is the great-great-granddaughter of Pan, and the granddaughter of the river Po. Aminta calls her, conceitedly, 'honour of the woods (*selve*) and ardour of the soul' (I. ii. 317). One's chance of identifying either with a woodland or a fire are slight. Yet such language has its own significance, its own precision, and its own claim to being poetry.

(iii) *The Golden Age and the Ages of Man*

It is when viewed collectively, in the perspective of a mental landscape, that the pastoral motifs assume their proper order and expression. Of none of them is this so true as of the Golden Age, an 'idea which comes perhaps as near being universal in pastoral as any'.[1]

This is another of those volatile motifs from the classical anthology that the Renaissance poet modifies to suit his own concerns. Not all antique or medieval treatments of it are pastoral, and not all pastoral treatments of it are alike.[2] Tasso echoes Ovid (*Metamorphoses*, i. 89 ff.), but his celebration of the Golden Age is not a wistful reconstruction of a time when everlasting spring prevailed, the earth provided for men's needs without being cultivated, and laws, injustice, foreign lands, and war were not yet known. On the contrary, its meaning is wholly metaphorical. The end of Act I is after all hardly the place for the epitome of the shepherd's life that this complaint is often said to be.

[*questa verga*]? Or are they for Tasso one and the same, gold-tipped [*punta d'oro*] as well as aflame [*d'invisibili fiamme*]? Or does Amore here carry a second pastoral attribute?

    [1] Greg, p. 5.
    [2] Cf. A. O. Lovejoy, *Primitivism and Related Ideas in Antiquity* (Baltimore, 1935), *passim*. Cf. R. Walker, *The Golden Feast* (London, 1952).

The famous stanzas beginning

> O bella età de l'oro (I. ii. 570)

are sung by the Chorus of shepherds *festanti e coronati* among whom
Amore mingles after his prologue. Their theme is not a return to
innocence but the loss of it in modern pastoral times:

> Tu prima, Onor, velasti
> La fonte de i diletti.[1] (I. ii. 609-10)

As the dialogues of Silvia with Dafne, and Aminta with Tirsi have
shown, a courtly code of honour nowadays constrains the love of
nymph and shepherd. Their age is clearly not golden any longer,
though it is none the less pastoral for that.

Dafne in fact teases Silvia for behaving as if she were living in the
Golden Age:

> Così la gente prima, che già visse
> Nel mondo ancora semplice ed infante,
> Stimò dolce bevanda e dolce cibo
> L'acqua e le ghiande.[2] (I. i. 20-3)

In a Platonizing and aesthetic world, abstinence is not a virtue.
'Nessuna cosa semplice può esser bella', says Pico. 'Dopo Dio comincia la bellezza, perchè comincia la contrarietà.'[3] In Dafne's view
the Golden Age is not an ideal world at all. And even if it is, she
does not in this instance mean the childhood of the world but the
world of childhood.

Aminta confirms as much by his account of how an innocent
childhood friendship with Silvia ended with the awakening of
passion:

> Ma mentre al cor scendeva
> Quella dolcezza, mista
> D'un secreto veleno,
> Tal diletto n'avea,

---

[1] Thou first, Honour, veiled the fountains of delight.

[2] Thus the first people, who once lived in a world still young and simple, thought
water and acorns sweet to eat and drink. (Cf. the tone of Montaigne's allusion to the
Golden Age in the notice to the reader of the *Essais*.)

[3] Pico, ed. Garin, p. 495: Beauty, i.e. contrariety, begins with God (*Commento*).

> Che, fingendo ch'ancor non mi passasse
> Il dolor di quel morso,
> Fei sì ch'ella più volte
> Vi replicò l'incanto.[1] (I. ii. 411–18)

The world evoked is that of the erotic Greek romances, Clitophon and Leucippe, Daphnis and Chloe. And it comes to mind as the vehicle for a remembered, and regretted, and yet not regretted age of individual innocence—the age at which Silvia is wilfully content to linger. Every single person, says Schiller, 'has his or her Golden Age'.[2] As a memory it corresponds to that luminous middle distance which lends wistfulness to the landscapes of the pastoral painters from Giorgione to Claude Lorrain.

Where this motif might be expected to carry a social rather than personal meaning is in Tirsi's long account of the Ferrarese court, which immediately precedes the Chorus itself. But the terms of this compliment to Alfonso II are heroic:

> Uom d'aspetto magnanimo e robusto,
> Di cui, per quanto intesi, in dubbio stassi,
> S'egli sia miglior duce o cavaliero.[3] (I. ii. 533–5)

Pastoral language is reserved for the ladies and the poets:

> Celesti Dee, ninfe leggiadre e belle,
> Nuovi Lini ed Orfei, ed altre ancora
> Senza vel, senza nube, e quale e quanta
> A gli immortali appar vergine Aurora.[4] (I. ii. 540–3)

And the Golden Age is not evoked at all. Ficino's letter about the golden talents, which are artistic and academic, may suggest why. Only Tirsi, the speaker himself, has certain attributes of Golden Age simplicity, 'rude manners', 'base birth', and the like. All his

---

[1] But while the sweetness, mingled with a secret poison, went to the heart, I took such delight in it that, feigning the hurt of the sting after it had passed, I made her repeat the charm again and again.

[2] J. C. F. v. Schiller, *Werke* (Stuttgart, 1904), XII. ii. 224 (*Über naive und sentimentalische Dichtung*).

[3] A man magnanimous and robust in aspect, about whom there is uncertainty, however many are agreed, whether he is the greater leader or knight-at-arms.

[4] Celestial goddesses, nymphs lovely and full of grace, Linus' and Orpheus' new selves, and others besides, unveiled, unconcealed by cloud, and such and so great as seems virgin Aurora to the immortals.

mere eloquence, he says, was picked up at court. This is the mask by which a courtly poet keeps his independence while flattering a patron—what Empson calls the pastoral twist to the heroic compliment.

In the inner life of the lover-poet the Golden Age thus stands for remembered innocence, while in the social life of the courtier-poet it stands for the inner life, or selfhood. In either case only a part of the shepherd's life is meant. Shepherdliness means that truth to his own feelings with which a lover or poet credits himself, a post-Socratic combination of the naïve and the self-conscious, the humble and the obsessed. Hence the uninhibited sensibility of Aminta and the sophisticated complaisance of Tirsi. Both seek to give the best expression possible to an ideal of service, whether of the lady or the prince, and by doing so to make a work of art out of natural impulse.

In the *Aminta*, as in *As You Like It*, the Golden Age is of less importance than the Ages of Man, and particularly that age, the spring of life, in which he is above all else the lover and the poet. It is the mentality of this age, the so-called aesthetic stage of life, that pastoral celebrates. Socrates calls it the 'beauty of the young, over whom the god of love watches' (*Phaedrus*, 265C). Kierkegaard calls it the 'immediate stages of the erotic'.[1]

Through Platonism the shepherd's life thus relates to a conception of existence, or consciousness, that may be regarded as perennial:

. . . a heightened state of mind, experienced independently of and even in opposition to all outward events, bearing in itself its own certainty and having in turn an influence on the form and interpretation of all our other experiences.[2]

Is this a definition of 'internal experience' in Ficino, or 'significant inwardness' in Kierkegaard? In the appeal of Mozart opera to the author of the *Either/Or* there is evidence of what Tasso's pastoralism means for the audience of the *Theologia Platonica* and its inheritors.

For Tasso the aesthetic stage involves the anarchy as well as

---

[1] S. Kierkegaard, *Either/Or*, trans. D. and L. Swenson (New York, 1959), i. 57 ff.
[2] P. O. Kristeller, *The Philosophy of Marsilio Ficino*, trans. V. Conant (New York, 1943), p. 206. Cf. Cassirer, *Individuum und Kosmos*, pp. 139–40.

inwardness of passion. 'Pronta allo sbaraglio', says Croce, 'e alla morte' (and for death):

> Silvia, le dissi, io per te ardo, e certo
> Morrò, se non m'aïti.[1] (I. ii. 427–8)

And if one asks what is the 'determining emotional pattern'[2] of the *Aminta*, the answer must be this: the will to love crossed with the wish to be pure, the urge to sing complicated by the need to know the truth. At some level of the mind sexuality and the singing voice are, as Mozart knew, inseparable, as are the acts of loving, dying, and knowing—the initiations. And the model on which he and Tasso before him compose the experiences that come of this is the familiar one of an initiation rite.

That the shepherd's life should have significance for a reader of Kierkegaard as well as of Ficino testifies to the persistence of the mythic in modern ways of understanding. As the Tristan is still the love myth of Europe and America, so the Orpheus is their myth of art; and the *Aminta* has a part in the formation of both. To the literature of passion Tasso brings the Renaissance Italian trick of sublimation, a variation of *dolce stil nuovo* and Petrarchism: romantic myth transposed to conscious art. Upon the religion of courtly love, which is modelled on Christianity, he imposes a Platonizing calm or *otium*—that antique wisdom of folly to which the age of Ficino pretended to have access.

Such a combination is feasible and even powerful because both the courtly myth and the myth of the shepherd imply a communion of the pure. This may be why the pastoral appeals to Puritan writers as much as to any other sort—to Lawrence, as well as to Milton and Marvell.

When myths lose their sacral and esoteric power, it is said, they become literature.[3] Yet long after pastoralism might be thought to have yielded up the mystery that inheres in myth, the illusion of it remains. This is the fascination of pastoral, the secret that makes it

---

[1] Silvia, I told her, I burn for you, and shall surely die unless you help me.
[2] Cf. Bodkin, p. 22.
[3] De Rougemont, p. 236.

the poetry of poetry—that it is not to be understood unless one grants that it is more than mere literature.

Like courtesy, pastoral is a 'poetry of conduct'.[1] But the conduct it concerns is that of poetry itself. So, as any Platonizing mystagogue from Socrates to Thomas Taylor would affirm, the power of the mythic in pastoral is not immanent in its images or ideas: it comes from the quality of the incantation. In the *Aminta* what finally matters is not the shepherd's life but Tasso's power of language as a poet and playwright.

[1] C. S. Lewis, *Allegory of Love* (Oxford 1936), p. 351. Cf. R. L. Stevenson, *Memories and Portraits* (New York, 1910), p. 232 ('A Gossip on Romance').

3

THE RITE OF ART

Arcades res divinas primi diis fecerunt.

HYGINUS

(i) *Esotericism and Theatre*

TO see that the *Aminta* is an accomplished piece of theatre one should look at it in the light of poetic theology. The theory of the Wisdom of the Ancients (*veterum sapientia*) enters deeply and with delightful effect into its action, plot, and language, informing both the love fable and the *intermedi* that embellish it. At the end of each act, the Arcadian scene unfolds into a different relevant motif from the Renaissance anthology of mysteries.

That Tasso held an Orphic theory of the arts is beyond question:

The miracles of love which the vulgar judge to be poetic falsehoods are true by the most exact mode of truth.[1]

As author of these *Conclusioni amorose* and other Platonizing treatises he belongs, like Leone Ebreo, to the later school of Ficino—a master who gave nothing, it is said, 'but a mythical vision of the universe'.[2] In Leone's *Dialoghi* alone there are enough readings of the Greek erotic myths to suggest a rationale for the *Aminta*.

In the *Discorsi* Tasso himself quotes a text radical to the Orphic aesthetics—Hesiod on the shepherds as keepers of the mysteries: how they were taught by the Muses to speak false things as if they were true and, when they wished, things that were really true.[3]

---

[1] T. Tasso, *Il Cataneo*, ed. E. Mazzali (Milan, 1959), p. 300 (*Conclusioni amorose*, xxxvi).

[2] L. Olschki, *The Genius of Italy* (New York, 1949), p. 272. For Tasso's knowledge of Ficino's work, cf. *Supplementum Ficinianum*, ii. 307.

[3] Hesiod, *Theogony*, ll. 26–8; T. Tasso, *Discorsi del poema eroico*, ed. E. Mazzali (Milan, 1959), pp. 531–2; Milton, *Comus*, ll. 476 ff. Cf. Olschki, *Genius of Italy*, pp. 269–70.

Here once again is the view of pastoralism as 'divine philosophy' informed by antique wisdom—an immanental view common to humanists of the Florentine persuasion.

In the *Aminta* accordingly, Tasso communicates with his audience through richer and more various means than are usually recognized. First, like Socrates, he describes the passion of love in some sort of figurative manner, 'expressing some truth, perhaps, and perhaps being led away in another direction'. This is in the scenes which rehearse Aminta's pursuit of Silvia. Then, after this 'somewhat plausible discourse', he breaks into a chant:

. . . a sportive and mythic hymn in meek and pious strain to the honour of your lord and mine, Phaedrus, the guardian of the young and beautiful. (*Phaedrus*, 265B)

The *intermedi* of the *Aminta*, as they survive, resemble nothing so much as the hymns of Orpheus *boukolos*. 'Ever to the herdsman have a kindly aspect.'[1]

It is as if four of these invocations, which address the Greek deities as different aspects of the One, were rendered by Tasso in the first person, as theophanies. In actual performance, as a *tableau vivant* with words, music, and dance, each *intermedio* would be like a staging of the *Primavera* or the *Sacred and Profane Love*.

Mythological *intermedi* were usually the most admired part of a sixteenth-century play. Those which Castiglione describes in a letter to Canossa about a performance of the *Calandria* at Urbino in 1513 were typically splendid to the eye and quite irrelevant to Bibbiena's plot. The *Mandragola* also is reported to have been performed with *intermedi*—nymphs and shepherds singing madrigals, quaintly enough.[2] As might be expected, someone who saw the *Aminta* performed at Pesaro in 1574 singles out for special praise the 'novità del Coro fra ciascuno Atto'.[3]

What is the novelty referred to? Is it perhaps that the extravagance of the *intermedi* is for once integral to the action of the play?

---

[1] *Orphica*, p. 59 (Hymn to Hecate): Βουκόλῳ εὐμενέουσαν ἀεὶ κεχαρηότι θυμῷ (l. 10).

[2] H. M. Purkis, 'Il rapporto tra gli interludi e l'opera teatrale nell'Italia del sedicesimo secolo', *Letterature moderne*, x (1960), 802–15.

[3] Tiburio Almerici in a letter cited by P. Serassi, preface to the Bodoni *Aminta* (Crispoli, 1789), p. 9. Cf. Greg, p. 178.

Tasso scholars have not thought so; and the *intermedi*, if printed at all, are usually gathered in an appendix. 'Die Zwischenakte kümmern uns wenig.'[1] Yet scholarship has in this been curiously reluctant to grant Tasso an imaginative power that in many a lesser poet may be taken for granted—the ability, while seeming to change topics, to 'realize the whole locally'. It is arguable, indeed, that the integrity of his Orphic hymns between the acts is exactly what makes the *Aminta* the paragon of court pastoral.

By framing his fable with a prologue of Cupid and an epilogue of Venus, Tasso announces the mythological terms in which he speaks. These evidently are not what a modern audience might consider merely poetical, since they also occur in the propositions of his philosophic treatise on love:

> *Amore* is the property of that which has being, and by *Amore* all things are made, conserved, and perfected, in nature, as well as in art and society.

> The beauty which the ancients called by the name of *Venere* is the efficient cause, not the material, though this may none the less be argued.[2]

In the use of these terms to open and close the *Aminta* there is a late reflex of the blow that Socrates dealt the art of tragedy. Once upon a time, says Nietzsche, the function of the prologue and epilogue was to dispel any doubt as to the truth of the myth being enacted. Then rationalism and self-consciousness set in, as witness the prologue of the *Bacchae*, and the mystery became aesthetic. Even for Tasso, however, the cult of Bacchic mystery in a sense survives. What the appearance of Amore announces, and the successive *intermedi* confirm, is a celebration of the power of love according to the rite invented by Orpheus.

This can only be appreciated by conceiving of the entire *Aminta* as a piece of 'living art'. The action is to bring the nymphs and shepherds, sceptical and naïve, young and old, into harmony with nature, with each other, and with the supernatural. The means of doing this is to find the One among the Many by a series of those

---

[1] Vossler, p. 37: We need not bother with the *entr'actes*. Cf. A. Solerti, ed. (Turin, 1901), p. 208.

[2] *Il Cataneo*, ed. Mazzali, pp. 251–2 (*Conclusioni amorose*, x and v).

analogies and transpositions which the language of myth makes possible—those movements between the articulate and the ineffable, the individual consciousness and the collective, which make up the art of composition. Thus the same patterns of contrary impulse occur in the mysteries invoked by the *intermedi* as in the love dialogues of nymph and shepherd: Cupid in flight from Venus, the immanence of Pan in Proteus, the dance of the Graces by which the unity of Venus unfolds, Apollo and Bacchus made one. But since these *are* mysteries they hold all Nature's contraries in solution:

> She knew such harmony alone
> Could hold all Heaven and Earth in happier union.
> (Milton, *Nativity Hymn*, ll. 107–8)

These are the ancient truths to which humanity in Tasso's view must seek to reconcile itself, not tragically, if with passion.

In the sequence of the *intermedi*, interspersed as they are with scenes from the shepherd's life, pastoral mythology takes on a sense and structure reminiscent of the dialectic in Plato. Without the *intermedi*, what is more, Tasso's poem would never achieve that magical effect of players and audience subsumed in a single moment of cosmic awareness which is the mark of the best Renaissance theatre.

The immortal who appears in the first *intermedio* is Proteus. He identifies himself with mutability, the transfigurations of the night, the changeability of lovers' minds, the sea of which he is the 'sacred shepherd', and the play itself, now in process of changing acts:

> Proteo son io, che trasmutar sembianti
> E forme soglio varïar sì spesso;
> E trovai l'arte onde notturna scena
> Cangia l'aspetto: e quinci Amore istesso
> Trasforma in tante guise i vaghi amanti,
> Com'ogni carme, ed ogni storia è piena.
> Ne la notte serena,
> Ne l'amico silenzio e ne l'orrore,
> Sacro marin pastore
> Vi mostra questo coro e questa pompa;

Né vien chi l'interrompa,
E turbi i nostri giuochi e i nostri canti.

The pageant of mutability, 'this chorus and this pomp', then proceeds.

'Pure sacred matter to transmute is thine' goes the Orphic hymn to Proteus in Taylor's translation. Though not a deity, says Proclus, he comprehends in himself all the forms of things generated. Protean mutability is the very dignity of Pico's man: in his adventurous pursuit of self-transformation, says Wind, he 'explores the universe as if he were exploring himself'. To comprehend its multiplicity, however, Pan or final unity must be kept in view.[1] All this Platonic theologizing is carried off as poetry with admirable tact in Tasso's 'sportive and mythic hymn'. A compliment to the maritime ambitions of the Estensi also obtains; a hint of the heroic to match Tirsi's solo on the glories of Ferrara. The measure of good pastoral is always the gap between the lyric simplicity of the words and the multiplicity of the sense they suggest.

The interrupter whom Proteo hopes will not appear must be Pan, sacred shepherd of the land. As the unity of All he would preclude the conflict and division out of which life and art, poetry and music, are first made—not to mention any complimentary heroic. It is not until the last *intermedio*, therefore, that he duly appears. For the present, the sway of Proteo over the mind of love and expectation of the audience sums up the action perfectly—as the shepherds' hymn to the Golden Age, which immediately precedes it, does not.

In the second *intermedio* the advantage of an Orphic turn of mind to the playwright shows more clearly still. As the complications of the shepherd's life accrue—love, the patron, the satyr, and the art—the Chorus prays for guidance:

Amore, in quale scola,
Da qual mastro s'apprende
La tua sì lunga e dubbia arte d'amare?[2] (II. iii. 417–19)

---

[1] Taylor, *Mystical Hymns of Orpheus*, p. 61 and n.; Wind, *Pagan Mysteries*, p. 158.
[2] Love, in what school, from what master is learned your so long and doubtful art of loving?

The phrasing of this apparently artless appeal is incomparable. Yet one's delight in it, and in the whole act it brings to a close, deepens when the *intermedio* unfolds. What has gone before is thrown into new and rich relief by a hymn to virtue reconciled with pleasure.

This both diminishes the shepherd figures and makes them more expressive. As an image of courtly life they are inward but topical. Now the *intermedio* reflects them under the species of Christian Platonic eternity:

> Sante leggi d'amore e di natura;
> Sacro laccio ch'ordío
> Fede sì pura di sì bel desio;
> Tenace nodo, e forti e cari stami;
> Soave giogo e dilettevol salma,
> Che fai l'umana compagnia gradita,
> Per cui regge due corpi un core, un'alma,
> E per cui sempre si gioisca ed ami
> Sino a l'amara ed ultima partita;
> Gioia, conforto e pace
> De la vita fugace;
> Del mal dolce ristoro, ed alto oblio;
> Chi più di voi ne riconduce a Dio?

What is invoked here—in anticipation, as it were, of the coda to *Among School Children*—is the sacred knot of love and nature, tying purity and desire, joining two bodies in the sway of one heart, one soul, making of human kind a sympathetic company and, after fleeting life, leading back to God.

Who sings these words is not specified in the text. Possibly it is Mercury, the hermetic courier of souls, as in the *Primavera*. But certainly their meaning is best embodied in the dance of the Graces, with its crucial pastoral rhythm of procession, rapture, and return.

The knot of love and nature is one that nymphs and shepherds have all been trying and failing to tie. For Silvia and Aminta the reconciling of purity and beauty to pleasure and increase remains a mystery, its truth obscured by passion. For Dafne and Tirsi, the practice if not the theory recommends itself. This complaisance and scepticism now take on a new aspect—and one that hardly deserves

Greg's jibe about the names 'the straight-forward London stage would bestow' on Dafne. The satyr also may be seen to have his part in love and nature's simple plan. Yet for all of these, submission to the sacred knot's sweet yoke means an act of less sublime simplicity than the dance of the Graces. It is a knot of Orphic and Bacchic artifice that Tasso himself is tying, though his chorus of shepherds affects not to know this:

> Amor, leggan pur gli altri
> Le socratiche carte,
> Ch'io in due begli occhi apprenderò quest'arte.[1]
>
> (II. iii. 452–4)

From the multiplicity of Proteo to the knot of the Graces is a dramatic complication: it anticipates a denouement by way of a crisis. Implicit in the figure of the Graces is a division deeper than that between Chastity and Pleasure and needing to be overcome by more drastic means than dancing with Beauty. The *Primavera* again serves to make this language of mythology graphic. In Botticelli's garden of Venus each phase of love has its darker side. And a chthonic trio of Zephyr, Chloris, and Flora prefigures the Graces with the unpurged violence of a Nature as yet unreconciled to Art.[2]

At the crisis of his life, accordingly, Tasso's shepherd finds himself at one with the nymph in a devotion to purity yet at odds over how to live it out. And by the end of Act III a consummation of their passion in a love-death appears imminent. Silvia is reported to have died, after the fashion of one of Diana's nymphs, while hunting in the woods:

> E questo è quanto
> Posso dirvi di Silvia; ed ecco 'l velo.[3] (III. ii. 228–9)

And Aminta resolves to end his own life:

> Or che fatt'ha l'estremo
> De la sua crudeltate,
> Ben soffrirà ch'io moia.[4] (III. ii. 253–5)

---

[1] Love, let others in the Socratic charts go read, while I in two fair eyes will learn this art.   [2] Wind, *Pagan Mysteries*, Ch. VII.

[3] And this is as much as I can tell of Silvia. Here is her veil. Cf. *As You Like It*, IV. iii. 150 ff. (Oliver, Ganymede, and the bloody napkin).

[4] Now that heaven has done the worst of its cruelty it will surely suffer me to die.

If the end of life is to make a work of art out of human nature—and Shakespeare as well as Tasso suggests it is—then the means of doing so may be death.

But, as they say in the mysteries, 'the thyrsus-bearers are many, but the Bacchoi are few' (*Phaedo*, 69D). And counter to the will to die run the responses of the other nymphs and shepherds, for whom Amore is god of love but not death. These culminate in the Chorus beginning

Non bisogna la morte, (III. ii. 288)

an expression of what is perhaps the classic pastoral sentiment— the one which earned it Nietzsche's eloquent contempt.

Whether a love that has 'no need of death' can be the *amore platonico* is doubtful. In theory, after seeing into the beyond the lover returns to move the world by the power of his clarified passion. The love swoon in pastoral—whether Aminta's or Rosalind's in *As You Like It*—means, if not death, then a vacating of the body by the soul after which it returns to a new life:

Ch'io vo' per non tornare. (III. ii. 280)

I pray you commend my counterfeiting to him.
(*AYLI*, IV. iii. 180)

In any case, an audience apt for Tasso's chosen mode of theatre, let alone his doctrine, would know a resounding answer to the optimism of the Chorus: death's never far distant

Et in Arcadia ego.

It is at this critical moment of division in the mind of love that the third and most enigmatic of the *intermedi* unfolds.

The gods descend and the *Aminta* reaches its still centre in a cosmic *ballo di divinità*:

Divi noi siam, che ne 'l sereno eterno
Fra celesti zaffiri e bei cristalli
Meniam perpetui balli,
Dove non è giammai state né verno:
Ed or grazia immortale, alta ventura
Qua giù ne tragge, in questa bella imago

De 'l teatro de 'l mondo;
Dove facciamo a tondo
Un ballo novo, e dilettoso e vago,
Fra tanti lumi de la notte oscura
A la chiara armonia de 'l suono alterno.

Grace and fortune bring these gods down to this fair image of the theatre of the world. Here they reveal the harmony in all things by circling together in a place of lights and darks to the clear music of an alternating strain. Again the speakers are not named in the text. Who might they be?

Tasso evidently tries here for an effect of both self-awareness and self-transcendence—an illumination—in the manner of a mythopoeic cultist. Nature, it is said, yields nothing without ceremonies: 'To know in a mythopoeic way one must engage in the gestures and ritual acts which bring . . . the desired communion.'[1] In this case these gestures are theatrical: song, dance, *décor*. Tasso simply reminds his audience at the right moment that they are in a theatre but that all the world's a stage; that the theatre can give only an illusion of resolving the complications of courtly life but that the illusion is a saving one. Art must always vie with nature, as Polixenes tells Perdita, for the perfection of culture.

This is a trick even Shakespeare never tired of playing, usually around the middle of Act III. By gathering up an audience at the moment of crisis into the artifice of the play and at the same time admitting the illusion, they can be brought to glimpse a reality behind as well as before them. But what for Tasso are the mythological terms of this penumbral illumination?

In some recognized yet mysterious union they must embody all the divisions of the courtier-lover-poet's mind so far rehearsed. Somehow the clarity of art must be seen to be equal to the chaos of nature, which it transfigures but does not deny. What gods would be equal to this occasion but Apollo and Bacchus?

If so, the logic of the mythic proposition argued in Tasso's *intermedi* may be represented as follows:

[1] Wheelwright, p. 169.

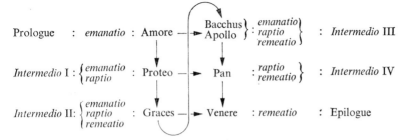

Amore, 'maker of all things in nature as well as art and society', issues in Bacchus-Apollo, by whose aid human culture advances; an analogy of Proteus issuing in Pan, and the Graces in Venus, two known conclusions of the poetic theology.[1] But the syntax of ritual takes the longer way round.

Whether Bacchus can be said to inhabit the 'eternal serene' might seem a question. But the answer may, as so often, be found in Orphic tradition, and in no more inaccessible a text than Macrobius on Virgil. When discussing whether Virgil's mythology may be read as philosophy, he cites the Orphic invocation which identifies Bacchus with Zeus.[2] As for the hymns of Orpheus, Bacchus figures in them much more frequently than any other deity, including Apollo.

On the other hand, what terms of the poetic theology would not serve to paraphrase the meaning of Bacchus-Apollo? Any suitable conjunction of mythologems, from Zeus-Minerva-Mercury to Urania and Clio, might enact the third *intermedio*. In this sense, the first principle of pastoral language is not the names of God at all, but *discordia concors* itself, a certain style.

(ii) *The Play as Subject of Itself*

The fourth and last of the *intermedi* makes an end of the fervid strain that develops in Acts III and IV. Pan appears, as Proteo

---

[1] Ficino, ii. 1559 (*In Plotinum*); Pico, *Opera*, 106–7 (*Conclusiones . . . hymnos Orphei*).
[2] Macrobius, *Saturnalia*, I. xxiii. 22: Ἀγλαὲ Ζεῦ Διόνυσε, πάτερ πόντου, πάτερ αἴης: O glorious Zeus Dionysos, father of the sea, father of the land,

hinted he would. And what he proceeds to do, with a delightful nonchalance, is dismiss the initiates:

> Itene, o mesti amanti, o donne liete,
> Ch'è tempo omai di placida quïete:
> Itene co 'l silenzio, ite co 'l sonno,
> Mentre versa papaveri e vïole
> La notte, e fugge il sole.
> E se i pensieri in voi dormir non ponno,
> Sian gli affanni amorosi
> In vece a voi de placidi riposi;
> Né miri il vostro pianto aurora o luna.
> Il gran Pan vi licenzia: omai tacete,
> Alme serve d'Amor, fide e segrete.[1]

The play, he says, is over. And since Pan means the unity of all the parts in 'endless dance and melody divine', over it must be—at least as a mystery rite.[2]

As a fable the play is not over at all. Silvia has returned alive from her misadventure, only to hear that Aminta has thrown himself from a cliff in despair. At this she suffers a change of heart, begs to be taken where he lies, and the Chorus hymns the symbiosis of love and death, as well it might.

The effect of an *ite* at this point is both hermetic and cathartic. As in the Orphic hymns, Shepherd Pan (*Pana nomios*) means that rationality has dominion over the irrational: 'he is the monad of . . . all the local gods and dæmons'.[3] It is as if Shakespeare put Puck's epilogue, not at the end of *A Midsummer-Night's Dream*, but before the dreamers awaken. One would still be sure that the best in this kind are but shadows, but not at all sure who deserves the ass-head for loving wisely but not too well.

---

[1] Go, sad lovers and joyful ladies: now is the time for peace and quiet. Go with silence, go with sleep, while night pours out her violets and poppies, and the sun takes flight. And if the thoughts within you cannot sleep, may the anguish of love be yours instead of peaceful rest. Nor let Aurora or Luna look on your complaints. Great Pan dismisses you. Be silent now, soul servants of Love, faithful and secret. (On mystical silence, cf. Ovid, *Metamorphoses*, ix. 692; A. Bocchi, *Symbolicae Quaestiones*, lxiv: 'Silentio deum cole—Monas manet in se': Worship God in silence. Unity rests in itself. Cited in Wind, *Pagan Mysteries*, p. 20.)

[2] Taylor, *Mystical Hymns of Orpheus*, p. 34 and n. (Hymn to Pan); cf. *Comus*, ll. 974–5.

[3] Ibid. Cf. *Orphica*, p. 64: Πᾶνα καλῶ κρατερόν, νόμιον, κόσμοιο τὸ σύμπαν (l. 1).

By beginning the resolution of his plot with a call to self-awareness, Tasso implies the transcendent mystery of what has gone
before. He thus effects a sophisticated *recul platonicien*, addressed to
those for whom fables speak of other things than can be said in
ordinary words. Telling the fable of the shepherd's life is but the
pretext for other more urgent actions, one otherworldly, the other
worldly: proving the immanence of Pan in Proteus and imposing on
life at court the sacral unity of art.

Shakespeare's pastoralism is never as radically mystical as this.
But he has devices comparable to the *intermedio* of Pan for making a
play the subject of itself. And for him as for Tasso, what begins in
the love passion continues as poetic theology and ends in aesthetic
unity. All pastoral aspires to the function of epithalamion, a Platonic
dream of having life every way.

Except to an audience of adepts, the art of much that Tasso does
in the *Aminta* must go for nothing. But of what Renaissance artist
may this not be said? The commentaries usually deprecate the final
act of the *Aminta*, calling it slight or perfunctory. And without an
understanding that pastoral is esoteric and so deprecates itself, its
wit can have little appeal.

The Act consists simply of an account given to the Chorus by
the old shepherd Elpino of Silvia's reunion with Aminta as he lay
senseless at the foot of the cliff:

> Ma come Silvia il riconobbe, e vide
> Le belle guance tenere d'Aminta
> Iscolorite in sì leggiadri modi
> Che vïola non è che impallidisca
> Sì dolcemente, e lui languir sì fatto
> Che parea già ne gli ultimi sospiri
> Esalar l'alma, in guisa di Baccante
> Gridando e percotendosi il bel petto,
> Lasciò cadersi in su 'l giacente corpo,
> E giunse viso a viso e bocca a bocca.[1]
>
> (v. i. 96–105)

[1] But when Silvia recognized him and saw the lovely tender cheeks of Aminta
colourless, so charming that the violet does not pale so gently, and him so in a swoon
that now the soul seemed to breathe its last sighs, like a Bacchante, crying out and

Having gone out of himself in the prescribed erotic manner, Aminta now returns to life, if not as an angel, then as an Orpheus. To such a mode of the poetic imagination allegory and play, as in the *Cupid and Psyche* of Apuleius, are everything.

Greg recognizes this passage as one of the finest in the piece, but deplores it as 'wantonly classical . . . effeminate . . . prophetic of a later age of morals and taste'. What may strike one in a yet later age of morals and taste is Tasso's considerable refinement on the prophetic style as found in the *Orfeo* of Poliziano. De Sanctis speaks with insight when he praises the *sprezzatura* of Tasso's poetry here.

The metre is hendecasyllabic, an equivalent of blank verse, but full of assonance and irregular rhyming. Frequently, as in the *intermedi*, this gives place to the *settenario* of three or four stresses, making for a flexibility and energy of style that look forward to the unique music of *Lycidas*. To this instrument, apt for the expression of a passionate languor at once formal and spontaneous, Tasso matches a diction in which rustic and conceited are one. A compromise between truth and eloquence, the cryptic and the lyrical—and vital to the future of pastoralism—is thus found.

In the few lines cited above, Tasso realizes the whole of his action. They imply all that Renaissance pastoralism means: an off-stage rite of nature by which Aminta's love is consummated; a 'maimed' rite of the Platonic theology by which a tragic union in death is controverted and the life of the soul in the natural world celebrated; an Orphic initiation at the hands of a Bacchante by which the shepherd's voice is purified; and a rite of art by which these others become a play scene of Elpino (G.-B. Pigna) telling the Chorus (Ferrara) how the court-poet (Tasso) deserves his patronage.

To expect such comprehension on the part of an audience is no doubt ambitious. Yet it is precisely the combination of a very simple action (*l'azione ancorachè semplice*) and most amusing conceits (*piacevolissimi concetti*) that pleases Almerici about Tasso's pastoral style. If one knew anything of *litterae humaniores*, it seems to have

beating her lovely breast, she fell upon his prostrate body and joined her face to his, mouth to mouth.

been that classical myth conceals the pagan theology of love. In this instance the whole passage echoes Socrates on the choice of a lover, with Bacchic qualities substituted for Zeus-like (*Phaedrus*, 252E–253A). For a poetic theologian, the allusion to Orpheus as victim of Bacchus also implies the ordeal of Marsyas as victim of Apollo—the pastoral version of the Socratic compromise. Where in Poliziano the examined life was Bacchic in mood, here in Tasso it is Apolline.[1]

The difficulty comes, not in recognizing that much more is meant than meets the ear, but in holding it all in mind at once. Making the mental effort to do so in the interest of the good Platonic life marks the dramatic climax of a play or poem in the pastoral mode, as here with 'in guisa di Baccante' or in *Lycidas* with

> Through the dear might of him that walked the waves.
>
> (l. 173)

The meaning of 'dramatic' has been handily defined as the tensions between a scenario and the suggestions thrown off by its imagery:

> [Such tensions give] . . . an inherent dialectic to the poem in which they occur . . . they tend to be ignored by the casual playgoer, whose mind is given over to spectacle and plot, but . . . the joy of a serious reader or auditor consists in responding as adequately as he is able.[2]

Yes and no. As inventor of a rite of art, the pastoralist seeks to bring his audience to just such a pitch of consciousness, and to do so he relies on as rich a fund of doctrine, motif, and style as tradition provides. But in spite of the above, which was written with the tragic in view, the most to be said for pastoralism is that it does not ask to be taken seriously.

The virtue of this mode is that saying is not assumed to make it so, any more than wishing. Hence its appeal to a brilliant, sceptical intelligence like Jonson's. It is a Socratic art of addressing the wise in a spirit of foolishness, the credit for encouraging which must go to Platonic mystagogy.

---

[1] Serassi, p. 8. For a classic instance of such theologizing, cf. Dante, *Paradiso*, i. 13–21.

[2] Wheelwright, p. 203.

Poetic theology always implies *serio ludere*. For Ficino to 'conceal the divine mysteries everywhere with figural covering' means specifically to 'jest in earnest and with most learned diligence to play'.[1] Hence the humours of the *Praise of Folly* and *Utopia*. Hence the airy, elusive tone of Tasso's pastoral climax. Tragedy, it is said, offers relief through the death of the hero. The catharsis offered by Aminta's Orphean fall comes quite differently—through finding the contradictions of the inner life temporarily resolved in the playful art of language.

Rank mystagogy, as so often in the Renaissance, can thus justify an 'eminently sensible' state of mind.[2] After rehearsing to the top of his bent the complications of the courtly life, how should a poet find the means to go on, if not by laughing them off? How does anyone who does not deny what he knows ever find the means to go on?

It should not be denied that in this very skilful pastoral recession of Tasso's a hint of unresolved crisis remains audible. A passion for purity that issues in the religion of art often verges on neurosis:

Haec eadem ut sciret quid non faciebat Amyntas?[3]

(*Bucolics*, ii. 135)

After such knowledge, what forgiveness? Let us say that this provides a modern audience with the authentic mannerist *frisson*.

The final chorus of the *Aminta* wittily combines the *dulce amarum* of lovesong with the learned humour of *serio ludere*:

Non so se il molto amaro. . . .[4] (v. i. 140)

The rite of love becomes subsumed in the rite of art, as in a parallel passage of the *Cortegiano* (III. liv). And as in the sequence of *intermedi* the Graces give place to Bacchus-Apollo, so the threefold rhythm of pastoral action now sounds twofold.

---

[1] Ficino, ii. 1137: 'ubique divina mysteria figuris involucrisque obtegere, . . . iocari serio, et studiosissime ludere' (*In Parmenidem*). Cf. Leone Ebreo, *Dialoghi d'amore*, ed. S. Caramella (Bari, 1929), pp. 101–2; Ficino, ii. 1129 (*Proœmium in Commentaria Platonis ad Laurentium*).

[2] Wind, *Pagan Mysteries*, p. 176.

[3] To know this [art of the oaten flute] what would Amyntas not do?

[4] I do not know if the great bitterness [he has suffered] . . . can be wholly made sweet by any present grace.

If Tasso's logic is indeed a movement between the Many and the One, multiplicity and unity, then duality may also be expected to emerge; as two comes between three and one. Body and soul, beauty and time, life and death, purity and pleasure, love and poetry, nature and art—the dualities of his meaning accumulate and, like those of his style, *dulce amarum* and *serio ludere*, in time become dominant. It would be interesting to see a musical translation of his threefold, twofold logic.

The unity in which he comes to rest is in mythological terms Venus. And the epilogue of Venere provides the extreme case of *serio ludere* or the play as subject of itself. That the love goddess should preside over the close of such a fable comes as no surprise. Hers is the ideal unity, invoked, unfolded, and transposed throughout. Yet there is nothing mystical about the sophisticated little complaint Tasso gives her:

> Ditemi, ov'è il mio figlio?[1] (Epilogue, l. 42)

The face of the play has long since turned from the beyond to the here and now.

Venere has more than a little of the courtesan about her, Aphrodite Pandemus, as in the *Symposium* (180E), though her pose is that of a *mater dolorosa*. After the more sublime moments of Aminta's transfiguration she faces the audience with complete inscrutability. And when she turns away, leaving the audience with itself—

> Ma, poi che no 'l trovo[2] (Epilogue, l. 146)—

what she concludes is not an esoteric rite but an entertainment. For the initiate, however, whom nothing can drive from the feast, this last teasing gesture may only confirm the prevalence of mystery. 'Ecce tibi rettuli quae, quamvis audita, ignores tamen necesse est.'[3]

From the *Orfeo* to the *Aminta* is not, by the standards of experiment set in the Renaissance, very far; and after the *Aminta* the most interesting developments in pastoral occur in other idioms than the Italian—in English poetry and in the prose of D'Urfé and Cervantes.

---

[1] Tell me, where is my son?
[2] But since I do not find him here.
[3] Apuleius, *Metamorphoses*, xi. 23: Behold, I have told you things which, although you have heard them, you must yet not know.

But it is far enough to establish the pastoral as a whole literary mode, with an ethos and style of its own, and available to poets of quite differing temperaments, the Florentine and the Neapolitan. Now, what modifications of it would a poet with a talent equal to Tasso's and working in the English theatre of the 1580s see fit to make?

Presumably his effort would be all towards a more vivid rendering of that worldly life against which the otherworldliness of pastoral is always set—towards a greater variety of plot and character, a more circumstantial reality. This, at least, is what one finds in Lyly, in Peele, in Shakespeare—the pastoral play following the fortunes of the Renaissance at large, from Ferrara to London, and from the lesser Elizabethans to the greater.[1]

But the trouble with questions and answers of this sort is that they are determined by what one already believes to have happened —evolution, or a cultural process. A question of usage, on the other hand, might lead to a new composition of what is known about Shakespeare. The question I shall answer therefore concerns, not literary history, but the language of criticism. It is this: Does an account of the pastoralism of the *Aminta* not apply equally and tellingly to certain of Shakespeare's early comedies?

[1] In the Italian theatre of the period a similar modification of the pastoral *personae* occurs, e.g. R. Gualterotti, *La Verginia*, Florence, 1584, and G. Leoni, *Roselmina*, Venice, 1595. Cf. L. G. Clubb, *Catalogue of Italian Plays 1500–1700 in the Folger Library*, forthcoming, 1968.

II

THE PASTORALISM OF
SHAKESPEARE'S EARLY COMEDIES

———◆———

4

THE TWO GENTLEMEN OF VERONA: ARCADES AMBO

Der Sinn für Wahrheit und Reinheit verlangt den 'Cultismus' der Sprache als das einzig gemäße Ausdrucksmittel.
CASSIRER

(i) The Folly of Loving

To a speculative reader of what remains the standard history of the subject in English, the following sentence comes as a surprise:

The pastoral tradition . . . finally reached this country in three main streams, the eclogue borrowed by Spenser from Marot, the romance suggested to Sidney by Montemayor, and the drama imitated by Daniel from Tasso and Guarini.[1]

What is surprising is that the playwright named with Spenser and Sidney in this context is Daniel and not Shakespeare.

The imitations of Italian pastoral that earn Daniel mention here, the *Queen's Arcadia* (1605) and the *Hymen's Triumph* (1614), do not belong with the *Shepheardes Calender* and the *Arcadia* to the reign of Elizabeth and the first flood of English pastoralism at all. Yet when the *Aminta* was played at Ferrara by the *Gelosi* under Tasso's direction Shakespeare was only nine years old. The same company had visited Paris with the play before he was ten. By 1584 a French version was in print. And by 1591 the *Aminta* was known and had been imitated all over Europe as part of the concurrent vogues of things Italian and things pastoral, and 'translated' into English by

---

[1] Greg, p. 215. Cf. V. M. Jeffrey, 'Italian and English Pastoral Drama of the Renaissance', *Modern Language Review*, xix (1924), p. 57. Also A. Fraunce, *The Arcadian Rhetorike* [1588], ed. E. Seaton (Oxford, 1950), where the *Aminta* prominently figures; C. P. Brand, *Torquato Tasso* (Cambridge, 1965), pp. 277-8.

Abraham Fraunce. By this time even the *Pastor fido* (1581–90), Guarini's inferior but more ambitious and finally more influential model of the *Aminta*, had been published in London, though not as yet in translation.

What of Shakespeare and his response to this pervasive literary fashion? Polonius, speaking presumably of the London stage in the 1590s, mentions it in the same breath with tragedy, comedy, and history. It is as likely that the most gifted and eclectic playwright of the decade should have known the tradition the *Aminta* epitomizes and made use of it in his comedies, as that later, in his tragedies, he should have used the *Essais* of Montaigne.

Not that the comedies are the earliest of his plays in which pastoralism appears. In the histories there is at least one important pastoral theme among the cluster of commonplaces concerning Fortune, Nature, and the Prince: it has been termed 'the rejection of the aspiring mind'.[1] It is central to the Henry VI trilogy, as witness the scene on Towton Field (II. v); and Shakespeare continues to develop it, more satisfyingly than anywhere perhaps in *Henry IV*.

But there is in the histories another notable instance of the centrality of pastoralism: the garden scene in *Richard II* (III. iv). This relates, as has been said, to the 'Renaissance habit of seeing the fields, the creatures, the trees, the hedgerows eloquent of higher mysteries—all that method of perception which owed [so] much to Plato'.[2] And it is this aspect of the tradition—a Neo-Platonic landscape of the mind, mythopoeically conceived, as by Tasso in his *Aminta*—that appears to have been the model for Shakespeare's originative experiments in romantic comedy during the 1590s. Unconstrained by neo-classical taste and encouraged by the example of Lyly, his 'pastoral-comical' begins to appear: imperfectly in the *Two Gentlemen*, but with improvement in *Love's Labour's Lost, A Midsummer-Night's Dream*, and *As You Like It*, which are still landscapes, and with growing freedom from the one mode in the *Merchant of*

[1] Smith, p. 10.
[2] P. Ure, ed., *King Richard II* (London, 1961), pp. li–lvii. Cf. Erasmus, *Convivium Religiosum*; *The Colloquies of Erasmus*, trans. C. R. Thompson (Chicago, 1965), pp. 48–78.

Venice, the *Merry Wives of Windsor*, *Much Ado About Nothing*, and *Twelfth Night*, all of which have their pastoral aspects.[1] The pastoralism of Tasso's *Aminta*, as I understand it, is a whole mode of the Platonizing and mythological imagination. It represents the accommodating of the Socratic idea of the good interior life to the Renaissance literary myth of the courtier-lover-poet. Thus its chief concerns are the psychology of the love passion, the mysteries which the Florentine Platonists professed to find in Greek myth, and the celebration of a rite of art and nature, Apollo and Bacchus, by which the contradictions of the courtly mind are for an ideal moment reconciled and transcended. And the more familiar pastoral symbolism of shepherd, nymph, and satyr, like the mythological figures of the *intermedi* of the *Aminta*, make part of that poetic theology of the One and the Many, or Pan brought out of Proteus, which informs so much Renaissance art from Botticelli to Marvell.

In this symbolism, as well as in action and theme, rhythm and tone, the *Two Gentlemen* echoes the pastoralism of the *Aminta*. What, for instance, does Shakespeare invoke in Proteus' first soliloquy,

> He after honour hunts, I after love, (I. i. 63)

if not the pastoral-heroic obverse of action and contemplation? What in Valentine's last soliloquy,

> How use doth breed a habit in a man, (v. iv. 1)

if not that obverse of court and country which premisses the inward and more perfect life of a Platonic mental landscape? Both of these key speeches belong as obviously to pastoral tradition as the famous song 'Who is Silvia?' And following Proteus' soliloquy, though different in tone, what does his tiresome raillery with Speed on the subject of sheep invoke if not the convention of the courtier-lover as shepherd?

---

[1] For this chronology, cf. Chambers, *William Shakespeare*, i. 270–1; J. G. McManaway, 'Recent Studies in Shakespeare's Chronology', *Shakespeare Survey 3* (Cambridge, 1950). But cf. T. W. Baldwin, *On the Literary Genetics of Shakespeare's Plays, 1592–1594* (Urbana, 1959), p. 241, who dates *Love's Labour's Lost* 1589 and the *Two Gentlemen* 1590. This order would suit the view that Shakespeare experiments more and more freely with orthodox pastoral. The text cited throughout is the New Cambridge Shakespeare, ed. A. Quiller-Couch and J. D. Wilson (Cambridge 1921–66).

True: and thy master a shepherd, (I. i. 81)

quips Proteus, anticipating Julia's equally self-conscious allusion much later in the plot:

> Alas, poor Proteus, thou hast entertained
> A fox to be the shepherd of thy lambs. (IV. iv. 89–90)

But rather than argue in this way that the *Two Gentlemen* is conventionally pastoral, let me approach the play with a question. What is there about the foolishness of young lovers that attracts, and goes on throughout the 1590s attracting, a poet-dramatist of Shakespeare's gifts? The question invites a variety of answers, ranging from 'Would he had blotted a thousand' to 'No man but a blockhead ever wrote except for money'. The one I shall offer is that Shakespeare wrote the first of his plays on the folly of loving with conscious—if inept—designs upon that fashionable cult of aesthetic Platonism of which pastoral was the favoured poetic mode.

The world of the *Two Gentlemen* is clearly the Italianate courtier-lover-poet's world, translated. Its bible is not so much the *Cortegiano* as *Euphues*, but its religion remains courtly, amorous, sub-philosophical—the love passion Neo-Platonized. It is preoccupied with the experiences and psychology of the aesthetic stage, their meaning and value. Throughout, the love god hovers no less absolutely and puckishly than in 'mysteries' as doctrinaire as the *Primavera* and the *Aminta*.

Love is your master, for he masters you, (I. i. 39)

Valentine tells Proteus contemptuously in the opening dialogue; but by their next exchange he is confessing:

> O, gentle Proteus, Love's a mighty lord,
>
> . . . .
>
> There is no woe to his correction,
> Nor to his service no such joy on earth.
> (II. iv. 134–7)

Proteus, in soliloquy, reveals the complications that a love of Love gives rise to:

> Love bade me swear, and love bids me forswear;
> O sweet-suggesting Love, if thou hast sinned,
> Teach me—thy tempted subject—to excuse it.
> (II. vi. 6–8)

And the Duke misconceives in thinking Love's influence is to be managed or presumed upon:

> This weak impress of love is as a figure
> Trenched in ice, which with an hour's heat
> Dissolves to water and doth lose his form . . . (III. ii. 6–8)

> And, Proteus, we dare trust you in this kind
> Because we know, on Valentine's report,
> You are already Love's firm votary,
> And cannot soon revolt and change your mind.
> (III. ii. 56–9)

Again, under a serio-comic aspect, the psychology of the love passion prevails.

The two most telling ideas about love in the play are the folly of loving and the blindness of Cupid. These are evoked chiefly by the conceited language of the wit-combats and soliloquies which predominate over more eventful scenes. The essential connection in the early comedies between the Euphuistic cult of the word (Logos) and the Neo-Platonic theory of Eros which gave rise to it is well remarked by Cassirer in his study of the Platonic Renaissance in England. And while such a conceit as the foolish wisdom of loving may now strike one as a mere period cliché, its very familiarity testifies to (in his phrase) 'a shimmering many-sidedness', which Shakespeare also found attractive.[1]

Plato anticipates both the pro and the con of it in the *Symposium* and the *Republic* and, more importantly for pastoral tradition, in the *Phaedrus*; all of which Ficino gave to the sixteenth century in annotated editions and translations. For the school of Ficino and its many auxiliaries among the artists, the folly of loving becomes a notable instance of otherworldly versus worldly estimates of human experience, such as aesthetic Platonism typically seeks to

---

[1] *Platonische Renaissance*, p. 123 (trans. J. P. Pettegrove). Cf. *Phaedrus*, 231E, 244A.

explore and formulate. The exploration of the Many in search of the One, which Ficino and Pico take for the motive of their speculations, and Tasso for that of the *Aminta*; or the compromise between action and contemplation, which Landino undertakes in the *Disputationes Camaldulenses* and Raphael in the *Dream of Scipio*: each reveals the same syncretic impulse towards intellectual unity by way of the *discordia concors* of the mysteries. This means relying on the mythic element in language by which a union of contraries may be named and imaged, rather than on the element by which it may be verbally enacted, as in paradox.

The adaptation of the idea of folly to the courtly ethos, giving rise to the *virtù di pazzia* or courtliness of the folly of loving, occurs notably in the *Cortegiano* and is promulgated in the whole tradition of love treatises and courtesy books.[1] But for Shakespeare and his audience a more familiar recension would be found in the *Moriae Encomion*, translated by Chaloner in 1549 as the *Praise of Folly*. In this far from slavishly Florentine essay in wit and irony Erasmus exalts the 'higher folly of the inner . . . life' over the 'lower folly of ordinary existence'.[2]

The witty idealism of Erasmus and the Platonizing *facetiae* of the pastoralist imply a common theory of humour as religious discipline:

. . . there is a simplicity which embraces and transcends complexity. The divided mind . . . need not be self-destructive. Although the deepest understanding may not bring such experiences to harmony, or the play of consciousness give them a musical setting, these spiritual powers [of laughing and weeping with a sense of the transience of joy and tears] can at least place them in some degree of esthetic distance and relate them intelligibly to a pattern not quite crazy.[3]

Allowing for his scholarly and religious rather than courtly and

---

[1] J. C. Nelson, *Renaissance Theory of Love: The Context of Giordano Bruno's 'Eroici furori'* (New York, 1958), Ch. II.

[2] P. O. Kristeller, *The Classics and Renaissance Thought* (Cambridge, Mass., 1955), pp. 62–3.

[3] H. H. Hudson, trans., *The Praise of Folly* (Princeton, 1941), p. xxxviii. Cf. H. A. Mason, *Humanism and Poetry in the Early Tudor Period* (London, 1959), pp. 59–103.

amorous bent, Erasmus may be said to anticipate Shakespeare's conceited treatment of the folly of loving in the *Two Gentlemen*.

An interest in the spiritual possibilities of folly thus enters the English imagination with the Oxford Reformers, who went to school to the Florentine Platonists. It gradually loses its Italianateness at the hands of More, Elyot, Ascham, Mulcaster—the mentors of Shakespeare's older contemporaries like Spenser and Lyly. But with their generation its Italianateness breaks out again, this time in poetry rather than prose.

How deliberately Shakespeare, in treating the courtly folly of loving, adopts the attitudes and vocabulary of Florentine Platonism remains a question. But if one looks to the *Two Gentlemen* it appears that he adopts them quite deliberately.

To begin with, there is that fairly laboured allusion in the opening dialogue to a love myth which in 1592, according to Abraham Fraunce, 'is in every man's mouth':[1]

> Proteus: Upon some book I love I'll pray for thee.
> Valentine: That's on some shallow story of deep love,
> How young Leander crossed the Hellespont.
> Proteus: That's a deep story of a deeper love. . . .
>
> (I. i. 20–3)

The effect is recognizably that of *serio ludere*. And at so broad a hint from a new and knowing playwright, a responsive audience would, like the audience for Marlowe's contemporary poem on the same love myth, 'bid goodbye to the world of sober experience at the very outset'.[2]

Then, in the ensuing scene between Julia and her confidante, a similar awareness of fashionable doctrine is presumed. The scene corresponds to an episode in Montemayor's pastoral novel, *Diana*—itself an expression of Florentine Platonism[3]—and, since Shakespeare

---

[1] A. Fraunce, *The Third Part of the Countess of Pembroke's Ivychurch: Entitled Aminta's Dale*. Wherein are the most conceited tales of the Pagan Gods in English Hexameters: together with their ancient descriptions and Philosophical explications (London, 1592), sig. M4ʳ. Cf. *Two Gentlemen*, III. i. 119–20.

[2] C. S. Lewis, *English Literature in the Sixteenth Century* (Oxford, 1954), p. 488.

[3] T. P. Harrison, 'Concerning the *Two Gentlemen of Verona* and Montemayor's *Diana*', *Modern Language Notes*, xli (1926), 251–2; Gerhardt, pp. 179, 187. The

boys his Julia in the posture of *la crudele Silvia*, to the opening scene of the *Aminta* as well. Julia begins by telling over the names of her admirers while Lucetta criticizes them pertly:

Julia: What think'st thou of the gentle Proteus?
Lucetta: Lord, lord . . . to see what folly reigns in us!
Julia: How now! What means this passion at his name?
                                                                        (I. ii. 14–16)

Then she by turns feigns indifference to Proteus, refuses his love letter, chases Lucetta away with it, calls her back penitently, boxes her ears when she refuses the letter, snatches it, tears it in pieces, and chases Lucetta away again, all before going down on her knees to gather up the pieces while speaking the 'Poor wounded name' speech. (Compare *Much Ado*, III. i, *passim*.)

The response which Shakespeare at best counts on to this charmingly operatic epitome of the lower and higher follies of the plot—coming at this point in the play and featuring his heroine— must in some measure be dynamic, even doctrinaire, and not merely indulgent and detached: it must comprehend something of the *serio* as well as the *ludere* of a Platonizing attitude towards the mysteries of Cupid. The satyric must be felt to have its part in virtue.

The mystery in which the higher as well as the lower folly of loving most aptly and familiarly finds expression—both in Florentine doctrine and the *Two Gentlemen*—is the blindness of Cupid: a mystery whose meaning and provenance in Renaissance art has been amply explored by the iconographers.[1] At its briefest, the Florentine version of the traditional idea of the blindness of love takes the form of the Orphic paradox that love-blindness is a higher form of vision: 'Ideo amor ab Orpheo sine oculis dicitur, quia est supra intellectum.'[2]

Shakespeare could have known of the traditional debate on love's blindness from several other sources, including Ovid, who in the

connection between the Platonism of Leone Ebreo and the pastoralism of the *Diana* is here represented as peculiar to Montemayor.

[1] E. Panofsky, *Studies in Iconology* (New York, 1939), pp. 95–128.
[2] Pico, *Opera*, pp. 95–6 (*Conclusiones in doctrinam Platonis*). Cf. G. Bruno, *Opere*, ed. G. Gentile (Bari, 1927), ii. 486 (*De gli eroici furori*).

Metamorphoses argues the pro, and Chaucer, who in the *Legend of Good Women*, doubts that love is blind at all. But the conclusion he approaches is, as one might expect, more conceitedly Renaissance in style than medieval: it does not assume that 'any positive evaluation of Love would necessarily have to reject [this] blindness'.[1] For example, in Julia's soliloquy in disguise as a page, over the picture of Silvia, which she must deliver to her master—

> What should it be that he respects in her,
> But I can make respective in myself,
> If this fond Love were not a blinded god?
>   (IV. iv. 192–4)—

he entertains his audience with some such recognizably Florentine version of the tradition as: the aim of love, though not always straight, is none the less always true. The 'fond Love' of which Proteus is a servant, 'blind' though they both may be, sees with a vision which is above the intellect. And to respond fully to Julia's speech—in the light, that is, of the inevitable final reconciliations of the plot—one needs to be aware of the providence as well as the improvidence of Love's blindness. Otherwise her sentiments—

> Alas, how love can trifle with itself (IV. iv. 181)—

amount only to an insipid piece of moralizing.

There is no question, I suppose, but that the action of the *Two Gentlemen* is all towards the expression and reconciliation of opposites in, as Cassirer says, a common medium of humorous verbal play—Proteus with Valentine, each with his first mistress, all with the Duke; Speed, Launce, Sir Thurio, and Sir Eglamour included, if only their parts had not been abridged or Shakespeare had not overlooked them. The action is as predictable as a rite; its appeal is to a sophisticated secular ceremonialism. Love's blindness being above the intellect, loving Love and loving death (as Proteus and Valentine do) being wiser than loving soberly, a final reconciliation must be reached by way of the foolish complications of the plot.

---

[1] Wind, *Pagan Mysteries*, p. 57. Cf. Ovid, *Metamorphoses*, iii. 430–1, 517–18; Chaucer, *Prologue to the Legend of Good Women*, ll. 169–70. The latter is a Middle English *Primavera*, with everything from Zephyrus and Flora, Alcestis and Hercules, to 'Origenes upon the Maudeleyne'.

And these, in their unfolding, clearly conform to that familiar Neo-Platonic rhythm of procession, rapture, and return (*emanatio, raptio, remeatio*) which also informs the *Primavera* and the *Aminta*. Everyone agrees that a Shakespeare comedy unfolds in three movements, and their names may as well be taken from Ficino as from Northrop Frye.

This triple and ever more self-consciously aesthetic rhythm of action is syncopated, as in the *Aminta*, by the duality of the play's major terms: folly and wisdom, blindness and vision, mutability and constancy, shadow and substance; a witty ambiguity, which pervades the speeches of the clowns as well as those of the gentlemen, their mistresses, and the Duke. And presumably an informed audience would recognize the modal implications, the feel, of this rhythm; not only its predictability as ritual but also the aestheticism of the whole ethos it suggests.

(ii) *Discordia Concors*

An apt way of expressing the aesthetic motive of the *Two Gentlemen* might be this: that the virtue of Apolline vision is imperfect without Bacchic delight. This idea can be traced from Bruno, who made a mark on literary London in the 1580s, back through Pico, Lorenzo, and Ficino, to Plotinus. For present purposes, the specific form in which Shakespeare knew of it hardly matters. It is even possible that he was writing slavishly in a fashionable mode, unaware of the conventions he appears to invoke; though it is more likely that, moving in the Southampton circle soon after the impact of the *Eroici furori* on Sidney and the Devereux family, he more or less knew what he was about.[1] But for the present what matters is how an awareness of current doctrines enters into one's appreciation of his play.

One such doctrine which, as Shakespeare invokes it, affects the

[1] F. L. Schoell, *Études sur l'humanisme continental en Angleterre* (Paris, 1926), Chs. I, II, VI; F. A. Yates, *A Study of 'Love's Labour's Lost'* (Cambridge, 1936), pp. 83–136; S. R. Jayne, 'Ficino and the Platonism of the English Renaissance', *Comparative Literature*, iv (1952), 214–38. Cf. V. K. Whitaker, *Shakespeare's Use of Learning* (San Marino, Calif., 1953), pp. 96–100.

whole tone of the piece is that of man as a chameleon. The word itself crops up twice; both times in an apparently contemptuous context. Speed ends his mockery of the newly love-smitten Valentine with this petition:

Ay, but hearken, sir: though the chameleon Love can feed on air, I am one that am nourished by my victuals; and would fain have meat. . . . (II. i. 164–8)

And Valentine later mocks his rival in front of their mistress with the same allusion:

Silvia: What, angry, Sir Thurio? do you change colour?
Valentine: Give him leave, madam—he is a kind of chameleon.
Thurio: That hath more mind to feed on your blood, than live in your air. (II. iv. 24–7)

Poor Thurio does turn out to be a turncoat and coward in the end, when Valentine dares him 'but to breathe upon my love' (V. iv. 132). But here he clearly foreshadows Proteus who, by falling in love with Silvia, shows that he, too, is a chameleon: as does Valentine himself.

At this rate, all the gentlemen are chameleonic; and a play on the honorific sense of the word becomes evident. 'Who would not admire this chameleon?' exclaims Pico in the most famous passage of the *De Hominis Dignitate*, alluding to man's power of self-transformation into brute, into angel, or into the solitude of his own mind where unity with the divine is possible.[1] And only if one recognizes that the chameleon stands for the courtier as shepherd, as well as satyr, does one catch the effective tone, the *serio ludere*, of Shakespeare's early comic style.

The reader who becomes most impatient with the *Two Gentlemen* takes it for a sober morality about a faithless friend and lover who, in the 'green world' of the finale, fails to get the comeuppance he so richly deserves. 'There are by this time *no* gentlemen in Verona', fusses Q about the reconciliation scene.[2] Yet Proteus is no more the Callimaco-like New Comic seducer than is his mythological

[1] Pico, ed. Garin, p. 106: 'Et si nulla creaturarum sorte contentus, in unitatis centrum suae se receperit, unus cum Deo spiritus factus, in solitaria . . . Quis hunc nostrum chamlæeonta non admiretur?'

[2] New Cambridge edition, p. xiv. Cf. F. M. Dickey, *Not Wisely But Too Well* (San Marino, Calif., 1957), p. 45.

namesake, *il sacro marin pastore*, of the *Aminta*. The marine symbolism of his name is often glanced at, as in his own speech

> Thus have I shunned the fire, for fear of burning,
> And drenched me in the sea, where I am drowned.
> (I. iii. 78–9)

in Valentine's

> Forgive me that I do not dream of thee (II. iv. 170)

and in Julia's 'Poor wounded name' and

> The current that with gentle murmur glides. (II. vii. 25)

And taken together with Valentine, signifying constancy, the name suggests that Shakespeare's plot is not so much moral in sense as aesthetic, in the manner of Orphic pastoral: a matter of Jack given his Jill, Pan found in Proteus, and a unity of art brought out of the multiplicity of nature. 'Frustra adit naturam et Protheum,qui Pana non attraxerit.[1]

If Proteus were the only allusion to the poetic theology, this reading would be doubtful. But the text is a tissue of such conceits. Though hardly programmed in the manner of Tasso or Botticelli, they crop up at significant points. Besides Proteus, and Valentine and Eglamour (which belong to a related symbolic tradition, courtly romance), there is the name Silvia, itself a trope. And among the *tropoi* there are Phaethon, Orpheus, and Ariadne: all as sophisticated in their rhetorical appeal as Elpino's comparison of Silvia to a Bacchante in the *Aminta*—although Shakespeare evidently lacks a command of the poetic theology proper that would make him Tasso's rival in the art of *serio ludere*.

In order to annotate the first of these, the Duke's Marlovian trope for Valentine, modern editors have to suppose so sophisticated an Ovidian usage that it may well be Platonic too:

> Why, Phaethon—for thou art Merops' son!—
> Wilt thou aspire to guide the heavenly car,
> And with thy daring folly burn the world? (III. i. 153–5)

---

[1] Pico, *Opera*, p. 107 (*Conclusiones hymnos . . . Orphei*); cf. *supra*, p. 9.

Panofsky points out that Michelangelo in his drawings for Tommaso Cavaliere and in his poems uses the Phaethon image to suggest both the presumption and the humility of erotic love.[1] And here Shakespeare may be seen distancing and transcending the Duke's moral outburst against Valentine's love for Silvia by the same mythological conceit.

Again, there is Proteus' allusion to Orpheus in his speech on love service:

> For Orpheus' lute was strung with poets' sinews—
> Whose golden touch could soften steel and stones;
> Make tigers tame and huge Leviathans
> Forsake unsounded deeps to dance on sands.
>
> (III. ii. 78–81)

This prepares for the most effective, and problematic, scene in the play, the night piece to Silvia; the problem being why the most musical moment of all should belong to Proteus. It is the one scene in which Shakespeare successfully invokes the 'magic potency of the theater', seeking as Tasso does in his third *intermedio* in the *Aminta* to gather up his audience into the art of his play by reminding them of a reality beyond their own.

Proteus may appear at this point to be 'perjured to the bosom', but as the Duke observes, there is a mysterious propriety to his love service. His invocation of Orpheus implies, as in the *Aminta*, a ritual concern with suffering and purification such as no initiated audience would condemn. Like Tasso's courtly satyr, he is but an agent of the blinded god. What he does to his mistress, his friend, and Silvia has some of that virtue of mutability and self-transcendence which Pico finds in the Proteus myth itself.[2] And in the 'story of his loves', as Valentine calls it, one should probably see, not so much the shallowness of villainy, as the depth of an Orphean

---

[1] Panofsky, *Studies in Iconology*, pp. 218–20.
[2] Pico, ed. Garin, p. 106 (*De Dignitate*): 'Quem non immerito Asclepius Atheniensis versipellis huius et seipsam transformantis naturae argumento per Proteum in mysteriis significari dixit': It was man who was said by Asclepius of Athens to be symbolized by Proteus in the mysteries, on account of his mutability and power to transform his own nature.

passion for the true beauty—of sounds as well as bodies—which he anticipates in the speech on the proper service of Silvia and achieves, momentarily, in his 'evening music to her ear'.

Again, Julia's allusion to herself as Ariadne, abandoned by Theseus on Naxos but taken up by Bacchus and transformed into a constellation, sounds like further preparation for a final scene of selftranscendence in a landscape of the mind:

> Madam, 'twas Ariadne, passioning
> For Theseus' perjury and unjust flight;
> Which I so lively acted with my tears . . .
>   (IV. iv. 165–7)

This passage on 'our pageants of delight' at Pentecost has been read as an allusion to Elizabethan festival. But in context it is more significantly an allusion to that pagan mystery which informs Titian's exuberantly festive *Bacchus and Ariadne*: it comes in a crucial dialogue between the heroines, full of references to Silvia's picture and Julia's ring, blindness and vision, shadow and substance.

It is notable, indeed, that the three Platonizing allusions instanced here—Phaethon, Orpheus, Ariadne—all occur at a definitive moment for the character concerned. And each has a connection with the others through the mythology of Montemayor's *Diana*, as well as Ovid, suggesting that the anticipated response might be learned as much from pastoral literature as from the poetic theology proper.

In spite of Shakespeare's free experiment with it, the mode of the *Two Gentlemen* remains discernibly pastoral: a mythopoeic rite in which symbolic figures collectively enact a mystery of the love passion. Between Proteus and Valentine there is not so much conflict as collusion: 'Arcades ambo, id est, blackguards both.' The Bacchic proclivities of the one being the instigation rather than the undoing of the Apolline virtue of the other, they represent complementary aspects of the same resolvable mind of love.

Proteus plays satyr to Valentine's shepherd as well as Proteus to his Pan. The better love servant to begin with, he provides that 'obstacle voulu', as de Rougemont would call it, without which Valentine, the better lover in the end, would not suffer the privative, purifying, and ennobling experience of banishment to the forest. Even if one sets mythological symbolism aside, the character of Proteus still strikes one as being informed by a Platonizing idealism, as in the not very villainous soliloquy,

> Love bids me swear, and Love bids me forswear, (II. vi. 6)

a glance at the truth that men who seem morally most contemptible often enjoy the most vivid visions of the possibilities of human life. For a Platonizing imagination there is, in the ontological sense, 'nothing but good'.[1]

Shakespeare's ethic in the *Two Gentlemen* is thus modified in accordance with the aestheticism of the mode in which he writes. He still indulges in homespun ethical ironies, but they are merely an undertone. His objections to the aesthetic stage—for example, to the love passion as self-love—do not so much deny as display and qualify its values. For him, as for Tasso in the *Aminta*, Castiglione in the *Cortegiano*, and Plato in the *Symposium*, the purpose is to preserve, refine, and purify the vivid sensations and intuitions of youth, while outgrowing the mere follies of it.

The problem of Platonic love as self-love brings one from the virtuous vices of Proteus to the vicious virtues of Valentine. He resembles the Philautus of Lyly's *Euphues*, who 'being a town-bred childe . . . crept into credit with Don Ferardo', won the hand but not the love of his daughter, lost her to his friend, whom she loved, but, when Eupheus in turn lost her, was virtuously reconciled to him. The virtues of Philautus-Valentine probably owe something also to the Gysippus of Elyot's *Governor*, who willingly relinquishes the lady in question to his friend Titus, the Euphues-Proteus figure. But in Shakespeare's presentation there is above all a reminiscence of Philautia, or self-love, in the *Praise of Folly*, who, says

---

[1] Kristeller, *Philosophy of M. Ficino*, p. 356. Cf. J. Vyvyan, *Shakespeare and Platonic Beauty* (London, 1961), pp. 62–76. Shakespeare, like Ficino, enjoys the paradoxes of *malum*, in this case Proteus' 'villainy'. For a later variation on *arcades ambo*, cf. Bassanio and Antonio in the *Merchant of Venice*.

Erasmus, takes the part of sister to Folly and is giver of man's delight; a goddess no less ambiguous in her gifts than Folly herself.[1]

As Valentine first appears, scoffing at the folly of loving, he engages less sympathy than Proteus; and Speed is later permitted to mock him with self-love—and in fourteeners, too. In his conversion to the religion of love he still compares unfavourably with Proteus, who rebukes his 'braggardism'; and his most sympathetic quality remains his love for Proteus:

> I know him for myself: for from our infancy
> We have conversed. (II. iv. 60–1)

With banishment to the forest, Valentine comes into his own. But by this time too much play on 'self' has gone on—in Proteus'

> If I lose them, thus find I by their loss—
> For Valentine, myself . . . (II. vi. 21–2)

in his own

> To die is to be banished from myself
> And Silvia is myself . . . (III. i. 9–10)

and in the Outlaws' strangely mirror-like portraits (IV. i. 22–3)— for one to think of Valentine as more than the *alter ego* of Proteus.

With Silvia a familiar, generic pastoralism is apparent. She is the nymph whom all the swains commend. When Valentine first praises her to Proteus as

> Sovereign to all creatures on the earth (II. iv. 151)

he proclaims, in the approved pastoral manner, the art-like superiority of her beauty to nature's and to Julia's. She thus has the complementary relation to Julia that he has to Proteus, except that Shakespeare identifies them with substance and shadow, not constancy and mutability. And in the forest Valentine prays

> Repair me with thy presence, Silvia:
> Thou gentle nymph, cherish thy forlorn swain.
> (V. iv. 11–12)

---

[1] Erasmus, *Moriae Encomion* (Basle, 1515), sigs. E₈ᵛ, Lᵛ: 'Videtis, opinor, quantum ubique voluptatis pariat': I am sure you observe how [Philautia] is everywhere the parent of delight.

Because of its pastoral language, this prayer to a goddess seen in the form of the beloved sounds fashionably Elizabethan. But like so many of the pastoral motifs, it goes back to Chaucer, where after seeing Emily walking in a garden, Palamon prays to Venus (*Knight's Tale*, l. 1103).

Maria Wickert, discussing the forms that the idea of shadow and substance takes in the plays and poems, suggests that Shakespeare's audience would associate what is said in the night piece when Proteus begs Silvia's picture both with the Narcissus myth and with the myth of Pygmalion and Galatea. The former, as interpreted by Ficino, images the soul's preference for heavenly beauty over its earthly shadow; while the latter could signify, indifferently, either the happy or unhappy fate of such love.[1]

And if so, the appeal of such scenes consists, not so much in any interplay of character, as in what Cassirer terms 'the self-activity of the word': the word being 'shadow', and its self-activity the wit of its enactment as a conceit by an ambiguous Pygmalion and the two aspects of his Galatea.[2] Like Tasso's in the *Castitas-Voluptas* scenes between Silvia and Dafne in the *Aminta*, Shakespeare's art consists in rehearsing the ambiguities of a Platonic and pastoral conceit so as to persuade an audience to hold them in the mind's eye, momentarily composed.

Without the conceit of shadow and substance and the figure of the faithful shepherdess, Julia and the line of boyish heroines she initiates would hardly be conceivable. Her virtues are anticipated in Montemayor's Felismena, a character Shakespeare might have known also from a play adapted from the *Diana*.[3] And in the scene in which the shadow-substance conceit is rehearsed in her favour (II. iv), her potential pastoral grace appears. But as usual in Shakespeare, there is no radical doubt of the superiority of art to nature.

It is Julia to whom Valentine and the Duke must grant grace in

---

[1] M. Wickert, 'Das Schattenmotiv bei Shakespeare', *Anglia*, lxxi (1953), 275–6, 303–5.

[2] *Platonische Renaissance*, p. 123 (trans. J. P. Pettegrove).

[3] G. Bullough, ed., *Narrative and Dramatic Sources of Shakespeare* (London, 1957), i. 206: *Felix and Feliomena*, a lost play mentioned in Revels Accounts as played before the Queen at Greenwich in the Christmas season of 1584–5.

the forest, after she has swooned, recovered, and been recognized for herself; grace being here, as Cassirer puts it, the privilege of the higher nature, a free emanation of love which overcomes all barriers between individuals.[1] Julia's gracelessness, like the rest of the counter-convention, is the more delightful part of the play; the convention in point being that of the beloved as nymph—

> The heaven such grace did lend her. (IV. ii. 41)

but in writing counter to it, with the beloved as graceless boy—

> Why boy!
> Why wag! how now? What's the matter? (V. iv. 86–7)

Shakespeare finally confirms it.

It is in the lyric 'Who is Silvia?' that his conventional designs upon Italianate pastoralism best appear: the finding of an Orphic voice in which strains of Bacchic as well as Apolline virtue playfully and mysteriously mingle; the framing of 'some feeling line', as Proteus has it,

> That may discover such integrity. (III. ii. 76–7)

In this kind, the paragon for the 1590s is Marlowe's *Passionate Shepherd to His Love*, its primacy being acknowledged by Ralegh, Donne, and Milton. And the trick, it seems, is to catch perfectly the accent of the courtier-lover-poet as shepherd; the tone of the erotic whole man; sensual-rational-angelic, this-worldly and otherworldly; above all nonchalant, folly-inspired.

Shakespeare's Orphic song in the *Two Gentlemen*, like Jonson's 'Queen and Huntress' from *Cynthia's Revels*, depends for its life wholly upon mythopoeic convention. But unlike Jonson, who in his hymn to Diana religiously withholds the divine name, Shakespeare blandly chants it:

> Who is Sylvia? What is she,
> That all our swains commend her? (IV. ii. 38–9)

The effect is none the less of a deliberately playful mystification.

As promised, Proteus now appears in the priest-like role of one

---

[1] *Platonische Renaissance*, p. 83. Cf. A. Nygren, *Agape and Eros*, trans. A. G. Hebert and P. S. Wilson (London, 1932–9), II. i. 300–14.

schooled in the poetic theology as well as the religion of love. His first stanza invokes a theocrasy of Diana-Venus-Minerva.

> Holy, fair, and wise is she.
> The heaven such grace did lend her,
> That she might admired be. (IV. ii. 40–2)

His second invokes the triad of *Pulchritudo-Amor-Voluptas*, or Beauty reconciled to Pleasure by Blind love:

> Is she kind as she is fair?
> For beauty lives with kindness.
> Love doth to her eyes repair,
> To help him of his blindness:
> And, being helped, inhabits there. (IV. ii. 43–7)

His third stanza invokes the immortal beauty of the ever-changing moon—Diana-Luna-Hecate—and all in the holy name of Silvia.

What, indeed, is she? Virgin daughter of the Duke; nymph in a symbolic landscape, begotten by the passionate mind upon the divine book of nature; substance of the Heavenly Beauty; shadow; local habitation and a name? The virtue of *serio ludere*, more pleasing in poet than philosopher, is that when the question of over-interpreting arises the answer is always at hand: 'Behold, I tell you things which, although you have heard them, you must yet not know.'

'Who is Silvia?' means as much or as little as one is able to hear in it. Julia, as graceless boy, hears little but bad faith:

> You mistake: the musician likes me not. (IV. ii. 55)

But the Duke, hearing Proteus on the art of Orphic song, has already been moved to say, better perhaps than he knew,

> Much is the force of heaven-bred poesy. (III. ii. 72)

It is in context that a conventional pastoral voice acquires its full allusive range. As in the first *intermedio* of the *Aminta*, when the dramatic action is at its most divisive, a Proteus figure appears as master of the revels, envisioning final unity. He sings of nocturnal metamorphosis, transcendent mutability, the eternal round of procession, rapture, and return in nature and art, mankind and the divine. A doctrinaire piece of Platonizing mythopoeia, this Orphic song of Shakespeare's for a moment stands at the centre of several pastoral motifs, in this case freely modified ones: the two Euphuistic shepherds in debate over the beloved, one of them already *ne'i boschi*; Beauty, their cynosure, alone and melancholy in her moonlit tower; the faithful shepherdess, forlorn, transvestite, also melancholy; the ducal *geron*; the city-bred naturals; the satyric gentlemen of the greenwood; all waiting to be brought by Pan out of division into harmony.

Inevitably, one comes back to that frustrating last scene towards which the whole plot moves, but in which not all its complications are resolved by Shakespeare's imposing the unity of art. In turning to it, let me glance at the rest of his pastoral devices.

It is in the clown scenes that he appears to range farthest from orthodox pastoral. But they are integral to his plot, and an audience alive to the mode of it would recognize Speed and Launce as related, perhaps through pastoral *scenari* of the *commedia dell'arte*, to Italian clownish shepherds.[1] The mercurial Speed speaks a counter part to the chief dialogues in much the same conceited terms as Proteus, while the herculean Launce, foreshadowing Valentine, acts out a parody of love service with a dog. Crab must be the least courtly, passionate, Platonic, aesthetic dog in all *commedia erudita*. But even he distantly resembles Melampo in the *Pastor fido*, whose master cherishes him above the shepherdess Dorinda.[2]

The outlaw scenes also spell Elizabethan pastoral. Here, as with the clowning, the evidence is in Ben Jonson's *Sad Shepherd*; but even by the early 1590s plays on the greenwood tradition were being adapted explicitly to the pastoral mode.[3] And Shakespeare's writing confirms that he thought of the outlaw scenes as pastoral. What else should one infer from that quaint insistence, in the wilds of nature, upon civility and the arts of language as marks of the good outlaw

[1] O. J. Campbell, 'The *Two Gentlemen of Verona* and Italian Comedy', in *Studies in Shakespeare, Milton, and Donne* (New York, 1925), pp. 60–2; K. M. Lea, *Italian Popular Comedy* (Oxford, 1934), ii. 443.

[2] B. Guarini, *Il Pastor fido*, II. ii. 13–16.

[3] E. Arber, ed., *Transcript of the Registers of the Company of Stationers* (London, 1875), ii. 307: 'A Pastorall Pleasant Comedie of Robin Hood and Little John' (13–16 May 1594, Edward White, publisher).

life? In a laboured and obvious manner, they bring to mind that *discordia concors* of nature and art which it is always the purpose of the Renaissance pastoralist to rehearse.

(iii) *Love's Labour's Won*

Shakespeare is hardly to be credited in the *Two Gentlemen* with realizing the possibilities of the pastoral mode of drama. None the less, they are the possibilities he seeks in his own style to realize; and nowhere more obviously than in the reconciliation scene, which even his most sympathetic readers understandably balk at. Here, as elsewhere, Tasso's *Aminta*, with its satyr piece at the fountain (III. i) and 'return to life' at the perilous cliff (v. i), offers the best insight into the conception he tries, without benefit of *oratio obliqua*, to carry out, and the orientation he assumes in his audience.

The movement of *raptio*, which begins when Valentine falls in love with Silvia, grows when Proteus follows suit, and achieves a critical moment of self-transcendence and cosmic unity in the night-piece, should ideally achieve its climax in the forest: Proteus-Orpheus and the beauty of bodies and sounds being reconciled in the movement of *remeatio* to Pan-Valentine and the beauty of souls. But the climax, as it turns out, is not only inferior as poetry, it is also absurd: a revelation, as Chambers well says, of 'sentimental bankruptcy'.[1]

R. Warwick Bond, far as he is from thinking this or Lyly's style of comedy pastoral, is also perceptive in pointing out the Platonic and formulary quality of those much-criticized key lines in which Valentine, having forgiven Proteus, appears to renounce Silvia to him:

> And that my love may appear plain and free,
> All that was mine in Sylvia I give thee. (v. iv. 82–3)

---

[1] E. K. Chambers, *Shakespeare: A Survey* (New York, n.d.), p. 51. Cf. *Merchant of Venice*, v. i; *Merry Wives*, v. ii ff., for further essays in *remeatio*. Belmont is a palace of the mind, a non-rural Arcadia, locale of the mercantile-courtly way of life, the more

Their playfully cryptic tone—here it may fairly be termed serio-ludicrous—is the very quality with which Shakespeare seeks to appeal to an audience of initiates at every other important point in the play.

According to Bond, Julia fails to perceive their Platonic meaning and, supposing Valentine to renounce Silvia, swoons, bringing on her own recognition.[1] Proteus, who in the night-piece has said that she is dead, then responds to her 'return to life' in the same execrable Platonic-cryptic style:

> What is in Silvia's face, but I may spy
> More fresh in Julia's with a constant eye?
>
> (v. iv. 115–16)

Such a reading at worst absolves one from arguing whether Julia's swoon is feigned or not. And at best it confirms that the difficulties of the scene, with its woodland setting, love swoon, and Platonic compromise, are conventional. It is a pastoral metamorphosis in the Garden of Venus, a ritual imposition of the unity of art which—in theory—makes a play the subject of itself:

> Come Proteus, 'tis your penance but to hear
> The story of your loves discovered . . .
> That done, our day of marriage shall be yours—
> One feast, one house, one mutual happiness.
>
> (v. iv. 171–4)

This is the Shakespearian equivalent of the epilogue of Venere, Tasso's *recul mythologique* in the *Aminta*. And no reader of the Cardenio episode in *Don Quixote* need wonder what pastoral clench is being employed.

Certain difficulties of the finale may even be explained away by a pastoral reading: notably the inconsistency of the Duke and

inward and pure by virtue of its foolish dedication to love, friendship, and beauty than the commercial-legal way in Venice. Windsor Forest is Windsor Forest.

[1] R. W. Bond, ed., Arden Shakespeare (London, 1906), p. xxxvii. For variations on the love swoon or feigned death, cf. *Much Ado*, IV. i; *As You Like It*, IV. iii; *Winter's Tale*, III. ii. In *Merchant of Venice*, IV, *passim*, Antonio's tragi-comic passage with death may be another variation on the swoon by which the nymph or shepherd is fitted for the masque of Hymen, as in the *Aminta*. The mask of Shakespeare's pastoralism is circumstance.

Eglamour, and possibly the statue-like silence of Silvia. She stands for Venus in a mimic theocrasy and there is nothing for her to say. Of the Duke, one may argue that once lured into

> This shadowy desert, unfrequented woods, (v. iv. 2)

he has no choice but to see the truth of Valentine and the falseness of Thurio, his sudden clarity of vision being a foregone pastoral conclusion; though Shakespeare might have made the *obbligato* less perfunctory. Eglamour, similarly, has no choice but to lose himself in the forest so that Silvia may meet the onset of the Bacchic forces of nature alone. He is a sad shepherd, with a heart

> As full of sorrows as the sea of sands. (IV. iii. 33)

And instead of being disposed of by the Third Outlaw in a single contemptuous line,

> Being nimble-footed, he hath outrun us, (v. iii. 6)

he should have been allowed to say to Valentine what Milton's two gentlemen in *Comus* say to the Attendant Spirit about their Lady:

> To tell thee sadly shepherd, without blame,
> Or our neglect, we lost her as we came. (ll. 509-10)

But then, Shakespeare should have found a place for Thurio, and for Launce and Speed as well, in his pastoral finale. He had not as tidy a mind as most of those who write about him.

Let it be agreed, nothing one says of this scene, or of the play as it has come down in the Folio text, will make of it anything but a failure. But so long as it continues to be read, studied, and produced, the way to read it will be of interest. It has been recognized as 'the earliest . . . romantic comedy of England, and almost of Europe',[1] and conceivably it is a better play of the sort Shakespeare set out to write than the standard reading allows. This reading may be summed up, in Northrop Frye's phrase, as 'an orthodox New Comedy except for one thing'; the exception being the resolution in the 'green world', prior to a return to the 'normal world'.[2]

---

[1] Bond, Arden edition, p. xxxii.

[2] N. Frye, 'The Argument of Comedy', *English Institute Essays, 1948* (New York, 1949), p. 67. Cf. J. Danby, 'Shakespeare Criticism and *Two Gentlemen of Verona*', *Critical Quarterly*, ii (1960), 309-21.

In the appreciation of the mature comedies an awareness of the mode in which Shakespeare writes perhaps matters little—though in the last comedies, significantly, his imagination is more obviously pastoral than ever. But in the appreciation of the *Two Gentlemen* especially, it makes a difference that his mode is pastoral: conventionally pastoral enough for the play to be termed 'an orthodox *pastoral* comedy except for one thing'. The exception is that nominal Arcadia of *personae* and setting which lends orthodox pastoral its more intense effect of an interior landscape.

But if Shakespeare had designs on the nineties, audience for pastoral, why does his title advertise Euphuism instead? Leaving aside the fact that contemporary taste ran all towards experiment within the traditional modes—and Euphues is Amyntas in mufti—there is a perfect answer to this question (except for one thing). The play's original title was *Love's Labour's Won*, taken from Valentine's opening complaint:

> To be in love: where scorn is bought with groans;
> Coy looks, with heart-sore sighs: one fading moment's mirth,
> With twenty watchful, weary, tedious nights;
> If haply won, perhaps a hapless gain;
> If lost, why then a grievous labour won;
> How ever . . . but a folly bought with wit.
> Or else a wit by folly vanquished. (I. i. 29–35)

Unfortunately, the *Two Gentlemen* is on Meres's list under its received title. But, of course, there is always Dover Wilson's theory, never disproved, that the received text is an abridgement of a poetically and dramatically superior piece—which perhaps had the pastoral-sounding title.

5

LOVE'S LABOUR'S LOST: IN ARCADIAM AMISSAM

Weil du Dionysus verlassen so verließ dich auch Apollo.

NIETZSCHE

(i) *Hercules at the Crossways*

IN *Love's Labour's Lost*, the other comedy thought to be written for the season of the *Two Gentlemen*, Shakespeare relies even more evidently on the figural premiss of a mental landscape. These two comedies in fact form a pastoral medal, rather like Raphael's companion paintings the *Dream of Scipio* and the *Three Graces*. Back to back with Cupid's reconciliation of virtue and pleasure is set the choice of Hercules between the two.[1]

That such a comparison should sound far-fetched shows how hard the old gossip about butchery and horse-holding is still dying. If it were a question of a pair of motifs in the *Faerie Queene*, no one would be uneasy. But for some reason Shakespearians would rather believe that this particular poet made up his mythologies out of folk games and rural experience than the art tradition of his time.

Yet what is Hercules doing so prominently among the allusions of *Love's Labour's Lost*, if not standing at the crossways of life, as in all such allegories since Prodicus?[2]

> For valour, is not Love a Hercules? (IV. iii. 337)

Behind the hero lies the life of action—like the figure of the knight

---

[1] E. Panofsky, *Hercules am Scheiderwege* (Leipzig, 1930), pp. 37–49, 142–52.

[2] Cf. Xenophon, *Memorabilia*, II. i. 21–34 (*De Factis et Dictis Socratis*); Cicero, *De Officiis*, I. xxxii. 118; III. v. 25; Petrarca, *De Vita Solitaria*, I. iv. 2; II. ix. 4; T. Mommsen, 'Petrarch and the Story of the Choice of Hercules', *Journal of the Warburg and Courtauld Institutes*, xvi (1953), 178–92.

in the left middle distance of the *Sacred and Profane Love*. This is the way Hercules has come. Heroic action is similarly given its due in a line or two of the opening scenes of the *Two Gentlemen*, *A Midsummer-Night's Dream*, *Much Ado*, and *As You Like It*. From then on only the life of contemplation lies in view, as here.

King Ferdinand's first speech proposes the stock Herculean choice between an erotic and an academic way to virtue:

> Let fame, that all hunt after in their lives,
> Live regist'red upon our brazen tombs,
> And then grace us, in the disgrace of death;
> When, spite of cormorant devouring Time,
> Th'endeavour of this present breath may buy
> That honour which shall bate his scythe's keen edge,
> And make us heirs of all eternity.
> Therefore, brave conquerors—for so you are
> That war against your own affections
> And the huge army of the world's desires—
> Our late edict shall strongly stand in force:
> Navarre shall be the wonder of the world,
> Our court shall be a little academe,
> Still and contemplative in living art. (I. i. 1–14)

These sentiments would not be out of place in *Lycidas*: the heroism of a life of study. But the tone is both mock-heroic and mock-virtuous, another style of playful reconcilement altogether than Milton's.

By Shakespeare's time the choice of Hercules is well known to be imperfect—witness Ficino's letter to Lorenzo about the *Philebus* and the judgement of Paris; and Bruno rehearses this theory at length in the *Eroici furori*, dedicated to Sidney.[1] As with love and blindness, so with pleasure and folly: a Platonic understanding does not deny the folly of it.

Hercules has been much cited as the model for Elizabethan heroes —for Sir Guyon, Tamburlaine, Bussy, Antony, Coriolanus.[2] But to take this figure wholly for heroic would be to mistake the nature

---

[1] Ficino, i. 919 (*Epistolae*); Bruno, ii. 417.

[2] Smith, pp. 293–303; F. Kermode, 'The Cave of Mammon', in *Elizabethan Poetry* (London, 1960), p. 166; E. Waith, *The Herculean Hero* (London, 1962).

of mythology. Just as Socrates wonders whether he is a Typhon or some gentler creature, so Orpheus and Paris have their heroic sides, and Hercules embodies the shepherd as well as the warrior—a tradition to which the *Alcestis*, Theocritus' Idyll XXIV, and Milton's nativity hymn all subscribe.

This duality is a counterpart to the logic of *discordia concors*, the 'mutual entailment of the gods'.[1] If a myth fails to include an episode in either mood, then the missing one has to be invented, as in the case of a warrior Christ. In Greek tradition the combining of pastoral and heroic goes back to the Titans who devour Dionysos and so endow mankind forever with that twofold nature which Socrates confronts. For the Florentine academy the twin cults in which it finds expression are those of Orpheus and Prometheus.[2]

A single motif may inform scenes from the warrior's life or the shepherd's. The parting of the ways in a landscape—the so-called 'verlandschaftlichte Pythagoräische Ypsilon'—appears in allegories of both Hercules and Orpheus, as in certain woodcuts by the *Narrenschiff* illustrator and Dürer which anticipate Raphael's companion paintings.[3] But such a landscape always signifies the inner life. And *Love's Labour's Lost*, accordingly, makes a notable Elizabethan contribution to the mythology of a pastoral Hercules; a shepherd figure analogous to Orpheus or Paris.

Like the *Orfeo*, the *Aminta*, most of Lyly, and the *Arraignment of Paris*, this play belongs to the literature of compliment. It was acted, says the Quarto, 'before her Highnes this last Christmas'. The way of a prince, as Ficino tells Lorenzo, is to neglect neither *sapientia*, nor *potentia*, nor *voluptas*, but to cultivate all three *pro meritis*. And even in London, where the patron is a virgin queen, it remains a formula of court pastoral to compliment her on her universality.

Like any formula, the complimentary can be restrictive. It severely curtails the pretty little piece on the judgement of Paris with which Peele anticipates Shakespeare's Hercules play. When the golden ball is at last given to Elizabeth, this compliment is

---

[1] Wind, *Pagan Mysteries*, p. 163.   [2] Chastel, p. 175.
[3] Panofsky, *Hercules*, p. 68.

settly *conclusively* nothing but a pastoral clench. A better way of putting it needs to be found. Some ten years later the way Shakespeare finds is to turn the self-consciousness of pastoral to account as theatrical wit. The mythologizing in *Love's Labour's Lost* is as wittily theatrical as the opening stanza of the *Good Morrow*. The work of such poetic language is not always accomplished by the razor of articulation, as in Donne. It is as often accomplished by a veil of allusion and analogy, as in Milton.

> He feels from Judah's Land
> The dreaded infant's hand.
> (*Nativity Hymn*, ll. 221–2)

With this nonchalant turn a long and devious scenario of the coming to birth at Bethlehem of a dying ancient culture is suddenly composed in the manner of the 'line of wit'.[1] Yet the paradoxical allusion to the infant Christ as Hercules is not a verbal enactment. What it says is not done in the words but somewhere beyond them. Shakespeare's early pastoral language, with its Orphic combination of biblical and euphuistic elements, is of this witty yet mysterious sort—but shot through with travesty.

To an audience aware that a court pastoral is in progress, Ferdinand's opening speech plainly rehearses the pose of Hercules *in bivio*. And plainly his one-sided version of it will never do. No self-respecting prince, no Platonizing academic, could regard the claims of books and ladies' eyes as alternate ways to 'living art', the *ars vivendi* of the Stoics.[2] The only royal way to the good life is to have it all ways. So the failure of the 'little academe' is from the first predictable—from Neo-Stoic theory as much as understanding of the human heart.

How Shakespeare manages this foregone conclusion, while displaying all the refinement that pastoral affords, accounts for most of the interest of his play.

It is three-quarters of a century since Pater, who understood

---

[1] Cf. F. R. Leavis, *Revaluation* (London, 1936), pp. 10–36.

[2] Cf. Cicero, *De Finibus*, I. iv, I. xii, III. ii; *Academica*, II. viii; Seneca, *Epistulae*, XCV, 8; J. S. Reid, 'Shakespeare's "Living Art" ', *Philological Quarterly*, i (1922), 226–7.

pastoral, noted that *Love's Labour's Lost* is unified by the conceit of a landscape:

> The scene—a park of the King of Navarre—is unaltered throughout; and the unity of the play is not so much the unity of a drama as that of a series of pictorial groups, in which the same figures reappear, in different combinations but on the same background. It is as if Shakespeare had intended to bind together, by some inventive conceit, the devices of an ancient tapestry, and give voices to its figures.[1]

Commentators have been apologizing for its lack of unity ever since; for its 'episodical nature', the absence of an 'ordered plot', and above all its 'indeterminate ending'.[2] The fate of the unemphatic is to go unheard, but not perhaps for ever. Now may be the moment to elaborate a little on Pater's remark.

The series of groups into which the play resolves itself is pastoral and kinetic in the manner of the *Aminta*. The first seven of these, making up the *protasis* and *epitasis*, may be summarized as follows:

(I. i) Ferdinand and his courtiers in the pose of Hercules, inclining to *virtus*.

(I. ii) Don Armado and Moth in a travesty of this pose, inclining to *voluptas*: 'Comfort me, boy. What great men have been in love?' Moth: 'Hercules, master.' (ll. 63–5)

(II) The Princess, her ladies, and Boyet in the pose of Venus with nymphs and Cupid (*puer senex*): 'He is Cupid's grandfather, and learns news of him.' (l. 254)[3]

(III) Don Armado, Moth, and Costard in a travesty of the complete man, with the motto *festina lente*. Berowne in the pose of Cupid's corporal (Eros chastised): 'Forsooth in love, I that have been love's whip!' (l. 173)

(IV. i) The Princess and her ladies in the pose of Diana and nymphs, inclining to *virtus*: 'But come, the bow: now mercy goes to kill' (l. 24). Rosaline, Boyet, Maria, and Costard with Berowne's

---

[1] W. Pater, *Appreciations* (London, 1911), pp. 162–3.
[2] R. David, ed., Arden Shakespeare (London, 1951), p. xxxvii; H. B. Charlton, *Shakespearian Comedy* (London, 1938), pp. 270–6; O. J. Campbell, '*Love's Labour's Lost* Re-studied', in *Studies in Shakespeare, Milton, and Donne* (New York, 1925), p. 18.
[3] Wind, *Pagan Mysteries*, p. 90. Cf. Lebeau in *As You Like It*, I. ii. 271–3.

letter in a travesty of *voluptas*: 'Thou canst not hit it, my good man' (l. 125). Johnson thought such scenes 'ought not to have been exhibited . . . to a maiden queen'.[1]

(IV. ii) Holofernes, Sir Nathaniel, and Dull in a travesty of the *vita contemplativa*.

(IV. iii) Ferdinand, Berowne, Longaville, and Dumaine, again posing as Hercules ('Still climbing trees in the Hesperides'), this time inclining to *voluptas*: 'Saint Cupid then! and soldiers to the field!' (ll. 338, 363)

For the mode of their continuity to be apparent, the 'theology' of these Platonizing tableaux need not be construed at length. This is clearly the language of pastoral myth, and the theme is bivalence or division.

With his flair for an allusion that sums up a culture, Edgar Wind has fixed upon Armado's 'Bring him festinately hither' (III. i. 5) as the clue to Shakespeare's meaning at the centre of this plot:

> The canon-ball which so aptly exploded at the climax of Shakespeare's quip, ['Sweet smoke of rhetoric! He reputes me a cannon'] was not a new conceit for *festina lente*; it was conventional, and that increased the satirical force of the image. In all earnestness, the Duke of Ferrara, Alfonso d'Este, like Federigo da Montefeltre before him, had used a bombshell as a heroic emblem, a symbol of concealed power propitiously released: A LIEU ET TEMPS. In Symeone's *Sententiose imprese*, a book not unlike Bruno's *Eroici furori*, the picture of the exploding 'ball of fire' is accompanied by moral verses which are about as pleasing as the sentiment they express. . . . The praise of this engine of destruction as a model of heroic prudence . . . contrasts with the sanity and courage of Ariosto who, although employed by these masters of artillery, did not fail to contradict their flatterers. . . . But to the inventors themselves—Leonardo da Vinci among them —[it] exemplified the magical forces of nature, forces which man carries also in his own breast. . . . In Bocchi's moral *Symbola*, the ancient observation, quoted by Cusanus, that minimal spaces may conceal maximal forces, that the energy of a small spark is potentially that of a great fire, was illustrated—in the midst of Socratic images of

---

[1] *Johnson on Shakespeare*, ed. W. Raleigh (Oxford, 1908), p. 89. For the orthodox model of this toxophilo-erotic, cf. Guarini, *Il Pastor Fido*, Prol., ll. 72–5.

Silenus, Minerva, Hercules, and Venus—by a picture of the invention of gunpowder. . . .[1]

Queen Elizabeth, it is said, envied the House of Este the kudos of its tradition of enlightened patronage. If Spenser saw himself as a rival of Tasso, why not Shakespeare? The Erasmian wisdom of *festina lente*, maturing slowly and then bursting forth, occurs a number of times in the plays.[2] In *King Lear*, as in Montaigne (*Essais* I. xx), it is rendered as a Socratic meditation on death:

> Men must endure
> Their going hence, even as their coming hither:
> Ripeness is all. (v. ii. 9–11)

In *A Midsummer-Night's Dream*, as in Ovid (*Metamorphoses*, iv. 55 ff.), it is part of the Orphic mystery of love, expressed emblematically as the sudden blooming of the mulberry where Pyramus and Thisbe die. In *Love's Labour's Lost* it comes in as one of the mock enigmas of a comic eclogue beginning

> Warble, child, make passionate my sense of hearing. (III. i. 1)

Here, too, life is conceived of as a sort of listening.

Moth and Costard are Arcadians with only a slight difference. They stand, like shepherds, for the life of the soul. But their masks are those of Butterfly and Crab, as in one of the several emblems of *festina lente* that the Renaissance learned from Augustan Rome.[3] (Costard means apple as well as head, so it also means crab, as in 'When roasted crabs hiss in the bowl', v. ii. 921.) It is thus a travesty of a dialogue about the whole man, rational, angelic, sensual, that these two stage with Armado:

Moth: A wonder, master! here's a costard broken in a shin.
Armado: Some enigma, some riddle—come, thy l'envoy—begin.
Costard: No egma, no riddle, no l'envoy, no salve in the mail, sir.
         O sir, plantain, a plain plantain! no l'envoy, no l'envoy, no salve sir, but a plantain! (III. i. 67–73)

---

[1] Wind, *Pagan Mysteries*, pp. 95–6. The quip, or comic routine, runs (with digressions) from l. 5 to l. 64.
[2] Cf. Erasmus, *Adagiorum Chiliades* (Basle, 1508), II. i. 1; Pater, *Renaissance*, p. 108 ('Leonardo da Vinci').   [3] Wind, *Pagan Mysteries*, p. 90.

Mystical Platonism met the demand made on any fashionable philosophy: 'it combined the obscure with the familiar.'[1] The New Cambridge editors note that the curative powers of the plantain crop up constantly in Elizabethan literature. Why?—if not partly because of some such esoteric pun as in Ficino's reading of the *Phaedrus*, 229.

To an initiate the pastoral mode of this comic Platonizing would be at once evident. What modern reader ever doubts that this is first and last an entertainment for and about initiates? A fashionable play now three hundred years out of date, says Granville-Barker, 'it abounds in jokes for the elect'.[2]

But topical allusions rarely determine the sense of an Elizabethan allegory, whether pastoral or heroic. Neither the *Ocean's Love to Cynthia* nor the *Faerie Queene* takes its structure from the actual events reflected in it. In this respect allusions remain topical, as in *Love's Labour's Lost*:

> In the main plot . . . are reflected certain exalted personages. In the sub-plot are the shadows of their numerous literary dependents and hangers-on. . . . Moreover, the eccentricities of the more unpopular of the exalted personages—Raleigh and Northumberland—may also be hinted at in the fantastics of the sub-plot.[3]

Programmatic identification of persons and occasions, whether in England in the 1590s or in France in the 1570s and 1580s, rarely satisfies a reader of this play. Given a revisory playwright, alluding prudently to affairs he knows only at second hand, this is to be expected. Yet actual persons, including Ralegh and Bruno, do come to mind as one reads.

Provided one has noticed the mode Shakespeare works in, his topical allusions fall into place in the usual spectrum of pastoral allegory, from cosmic to local, as in the *Aminta*. Frances Yates has done more to make this apparent than Shakespearians always appreciate. As at Florence in the time of Ficino, pastoralism here

---

[1] Wind, *Pagan Mysteries*, p. 89. Cf. A. Marvell, *Hortus*, l. 31.
[2] H. Granville-Barker, *Prefaces to Shakespeare* (Princeton, 1947), ii. 413.
[3] Yates, *Study*, p. 175. Cf. W. Oakeshott, *The Queen and the Poet* (London, 1960), Ch. IV.

reflects life at court under the ideal species of a Platonic academy. The provenance of this Platonism, however, is French rather than Italian:

> A study of the 'Academy' and 'ballets' at the Court of Navarre, together with the policy towards Catholics of Henry of Navarre during the later years of the reign of Henri III . . . shows that Shakespeare knew how an academy could pass from an oratorical to a poetic, and, finally, to a . . . religious phase. . . . His obsession with the concept of 'universal harmony' may have more in common with the Platonizing politics of conciliation than with any of the more obvious philosophical or religious groupings.[1]

Whether Shakespeare's 'civil war of wits' (II. i. 224) refers to a Valois *fête académique*, or the School of Night and its critics, or both, the ethos remains conciliatory.[2]

Royal patronage of Platonic academies on the Italian model coincides with the dynastic struggles in France beginning in the 1560s. Aesthetic theory calls for a polite cultivation of all the arts and sciences—music, dancing, astronomy, as well as rhetoric, philology, and moral philosophy—while practical circumstance leads to complications of the academic life. A series of conciliatory fêtes are held with both Guisin and Navarin, as in Ronsard's first eclogue, taking part. These are sometimes matrimonial in purpose, as well as academic and political, but always inconclusive, as witness the catastrophe of 1588–93.

Syncretism spells pastoral. And the preferred language for these transactions is the poetic theology, vulgarized by the mythographers and incorporated into masques or ballets. A culminating instance of the Platonizing theatre that results is the *Ballet comique de la reine* (1581), an allegory on the Circe theme that looks forward to *Comus*.

---

[1] F. A. Yates, *French Academies of the Sixteenth Century* (London, 1947), pp. 264–5 and n.
[2] Cassirer, *Platonische Renaissance*, pp. 123–4. More recent scholarship likes to talk of pastoral as a poetry of 'rejection'; cf. Smith, p. 10; F. Kermode, 'The Argument of Marvell's "Garden"', *Essays in Criticism*, ii (1952), 229; A. C. Hamilton, 'The Argument of Spenser's "Shepheardes Calender"', *ELH*, xxiii (1956), 181. It is, on the contrary, a poetry of conciliation.

Shakespeare could have read of this tradition in La Primaudaye's *Académie françoise*, translated 1586. But like aesthetic Platonism at large it is part of a contemporary artist's inheritance. Between Florence and Navarre come the humanist academies of Naples, Ferrara, and Bologna—writers of dialogues like Pontano, whose *Antonius* at points resembles *Love's Labour's Lost*, and purveyors of enigmas and emblems like Calcagnini and Bocchi.

French academicism does not provide Shakespeare with his plot or character types—these come from pastoral myth and *commedia dell'arte*. But it does contribute the courtly ambience of his play and a certain diminishing rhythm of action unusual in pastoral.

(ii) *Mirth and Melancholy*

Why does *Love's Labour's Lost* end with those inconclusive songs of the cuckoo and the owl, instead of the usual marriage feast? In the *Two Gentlemen*, *A Midsummer-Night's Dream*, and *As You Like It*, pastoralism means that the wisdom of passionate folly leads to a union of lover with beloved in a moment of cosmic harmony. If the clue to the unity of *Love's Labour's Lost* is pastoralism, what sense does it make of the finale?

From the first there are hints that the audience should notice the actual process of spinning this fable out of courtly English life in the nineties. And given the self-consciousness of all court theatre, this is not too much to hope for. What else can be the point of Berowne's persistent choric remarks?

> At Christmas I no more desire a rose
> Than wish a snow in May's new-fangled shows;
> (I. i. 106–7)
> I'll lay my head to any goodman's hat,
> These oaths and laws will prove an idle scorn—
> Sirrah, come on. (I. i. 298–300)

> I see the trick on't: here was a consent—
> Knowing aforehand of our merriment—
> To dash it like a Christmas comedy: (V. ii. 460–2)

Berowne: Our wooing doth not end like an old play:
          Jack hath not Jill: these ladies' courtesy
          Might well have made our sport a comedy.
King: Come, sir, it wants a twelvemonth an' a day,
          And then 'twill end.
Berowne: That's too long for a play. (v. ii. 870–4)

By the end of Act IV, certainly, one should be taking a conscious interest in Shakespeare's original and sophisticated pastoral experiment.

As each witty travesty of a conventional tableau follows the one before and the faint but familiar rhythm unfolds, certain queries come to mind. There is no happy ending in view, either in the 'civil war' being alluded to, or in the ethics of the good life being invoked. No dichotomy of the virtues, whether in favour of the scholarly or the erotic, can satisfy the universalizing function of pastoral compliment and pastoral aesthetics. Is good old Platonic syncretism breaking down, as Holofernes seems to think?

Old Mantuan! old Mantuan!Who understandeth thee
not, loves thee not. (iv. ii. 104)

What will be the outcome of all this *emanatio* without *raptio*, this Apollo without Bacchus, this *ludere* running away with the *serio*?

The plot appears to turn upon Berowne's spectacular praise of blind Cupid, an Orphic reversal of Ferdinand's Herculean *askesis*:

Have at you then affection's men at arms!
Consider what you first did swear unto:
To fast, to study, and to see no woman;
Flat treason 'gainst the kingly state of youth.
                    (iv. iii. 287–90)

But love, first learned in a lady's eyes,
Lives not alone immured in the brain;
But with the motion of all elements,
Courses as swift as thought in every power,
And gives to every power a double power,
Above their functions and their offices.
It adds a precious seeing to the eye;
A lover's eyes will gaze an eagle blind;

A lover's ear will hear the lowest sound,
When the suspicious heed of theft is stopped;
Love's feeling is more soft and sensible
Than are the tender horns of cockled snails;
Love's tongue proves dainty Bacchus gross in taste.
For valour, is not Love a Hercules,
Still climbing trees in the Hesperides?
Subtle as Sphinx, as sweet and musical
As bright Apollo's lute, strung with his hair;
And, when Love speaks, the voice of all the gods
Make heaven drowsy with the harmony.
Never durst poet touch a pen to write,
Until his ink were temp'red with Love's sighs;
O, then his lines would ravish savage ears,
And plant in tyrants mild humility.
From women's eyes this doctrine I derive:
They sparkle still the right Promethean fire—
They are the books, the arts, the academes,
That show, contain, and nourish all the world;
Else none at all in aught proves excellent.[1] (IV. iii. 324–51)

But this is as easily said and as mockingly heroic as

Navarre shall be the wonder of the world. (I. i. 12)

Berowne would like to be taken for an adept in poetic theology, an amateur Bruno, though 'ripe for delight' (*Laws* 2.699D). According to Orpheus, Cupid does issue in the ultimate mystery of Bacchus and Apollo made one. But even a myth has its rites. And truth, like justice, should be seen to be done, not just said.

Berowne may talk about the wisdom of folly, but where are the signs that these men of France are not merely foolish (*Phaedrus* 231D)? This must be the only love comedy in the canon with no going into exile or *travestimento*, no dreams or swooning, signifying *raptio*.[2] Berowne again supplies the chorus:

---

[1] Cf. *Aminta*, II. iii. 452–4: Love, let others in the Socratic charts go read, while I in two fair eyes will learn this art. In Berowne, as in the *Good Morrow*, the Orphic voice turns metaphysical.

[2] B. Evans, *Shakespeare's Comedies* (Oxford, 1960), p. viii. At the end of *Love's Labour's Lost*, instead of in its middle phase, a sort of going out of the self and into exile is pronounced as penance.

Allons! Allons! Sowed cockle reaped no corn,
And justice always whirls in equal measure:
Light wenches may prove plagues to men forsworn—
If so, our copper buys no better treasure.

(IV. iii. 380–3)

For revels, dances, masks, and merry hours,
Forerun fair Love, strewing her way with flowers.

(IV. iii. 376–7)

But not the masque of Hymen.

Shakespeare's answer to the queries he invites is not a surprise—not in a play presented to a queen whose way with suitors like Ivan the Terrible or Ralegh was notoriously short. But what is novel is the way the logic of pastoral is allowed to dictate its own conclusion on Ferdinand and Berowne's barren premisses.

Act V consists of another series of conventional scenes travestied, this time on the theme of concord or reconciliation:

(v. i) A prologue in which the ex-war-man Don Armado, attended by Moth and Costard, plots with the arts-man Holofernes, attended by Sir Nathaniel and Dull (Old fathers antic the church and the law), to entertain the love-men with scenes from the heroic life (the Nine Worthies).

(v. ii) The masque of the 'frozen Muscovits' (l. 265) and its sequel, a verdict on 'folly, in wisdom hatched' (l. 70).

(v. ii. 485) The anti-masque of the 'three times thrice' Worthies, with Hercules and Pompey numbered uncanonically among them.

(v. ii. 713) The *Et in Arcadia ego* of Marcade.[1]

(v. ii. 722) The confession of Ferdinand, Berowne, Longaville, Dumaine; and the penance imposed by the Princess: not pleasure but the puritan path of virtue.

(v. ii. 875) The eclogue of Spring and Winter, introduced by Armado.

This completes a clever process of turning the play into a charming but mocking post-mortem on itself.[2]

---

[1] Quarto and Folio spelling (emended by New Cambridge editors); cf. C. J. Sisson, *New Readings in Shakespeare* (Cambridge, 1956), i. 104.

[2] Cf. B. Roesen, '*Love's Labour's Lost*', *Shakespeare Quarterly*, iv (1953), 425.

As his title suggests, it is a sense of loss, of something missing from the courtly life that Shakespeare communicates. What is lacking in these forsworn pretenders to the golden apples of virtue and the harmony of Apollo's lute is a self-transcending passion comparable with Proteus' in the *Two Gentlemen*. The inspiration of all their virtuous and amorous posings is not passion but mockery. And when you leave out Bacchus, as Nietzsche says, Apollo leaves you out.

The outcome of this mockery is therefore not Orphic delight but Orphic melancholy. Saint Cupid, bright Apollo, dainty Bacchus, Lady Venus are not mocked. Nor are prankish Mercury and cold Minerva, the patrons of wisdom. They do not descend. Nor does the god Hercules. In the last act one maimed rite follows another until the thin voices of cuckoo and owl embrace all and die on the air.

The playwright who expected his audience to take much ethical satisfaction in such a play would be a simpler-minded stick than Shakespeare anywhere shows himself to be. Like most pastoralists he contrives in the aesthetic manner of Platonism and *concettismo* to have things all ways: to run with the deer in the King's park and hunt with the Princess and her ladies; to exploit the mythopoeic *cultus* of the age for all it is worth and at the same time to laugh at it.

Together with delight in celebrating Euphistic values goes the virtue of chastising affectation:

Full of dear guiltiness, and therefore this. . . . (v. ii. 787)

In this contradiction one hears at times the inimitable Shake-spearian undertone: 'A plague on both your houses', Ralegh and Essex, shepherd and nymph, knight and scholar. This comes out most clearly in the final anarchies of cuckoo and owl, but it gathers volume throughout the act, mostly in the phrases of the pedant, the boy, the fool, and the braggart:

Holofernes [Judas Maccabeus]: This is not generous, not gentle, not humble. (v. ii. 626)

Costard [of Sir Nathaniel as Alexander]: There, an't shall please you, a foolish mild man—an honest man, look you, and soon dashed. (v. ii. 566–8)

Moth [as Hercules]: Keep some state in thy exit, and vanish.
(v. ii. 589)
Costard [as Pompey]: 'Tis not so much worth; but I hope I was
perfect. I made a little fault in 'Great'. (v. ii. 555–6)
Armado [as Hector]: The sweet war-man is dead and rotten—sweet
chucks, beat not the bones of the buried: when he breathed, he
was a man. (v. ii. 659–61)

This last is not the only haunting piece of eloquence given to
Armado:

I have seen the day of wrong through the little hole of discretion,
and I will right myself like a soldier. (v. ii. 720–1)

And for all his extravagance, it is Armado, as master of the revels,
who finally emerges as the voice of the play.

The one usually taken to be Shakespeare's spokesman is of course
Berowne, who crosses words first with Hercules, then Cupid, and
finally forswears 'taffeta phrases' for 'russet yeas and honest kersey
noes'. All very straightforward and common sense. If it were not for
Berowne every moralist would have to think this play 'unworthy of
our Poet'.[1] Yet as much can be said—in a different vein—for the
central importance of Armado.

Holofernes calls him 'thrasonical' (v. i. 12) and Berowne 'the
braggart' (v. ii. 539), and since in the sub-plot Shakespeare may
have certain masks of the *commedia dell'arte* in mind, the name sticks.
The braggart captain of the *scenari* sometimes turns up in Arcadia,
in one instance posing as Cupid. But Don Armado belongs—if at
all—to a special class of *capitano*, the Euphuistic, like Andreini's
Spavento, who is hardly a braggart at all.[2]

What does Armado brag about? He is said to be

One who the music of his own vain tongue
Doth ravish like enchanting harmony. (I. i. 166–7)

In Arcadian Navarre that puts him in the best company. The sense
of truth and purity, says Cassirer, calls for a cult of language as its

[1] *Johnson on Shakespeare*, p. 89.
[2] Campbell, '*Love's Labour's Lost* Re-studied', pp. 22–33; E. K. Chambers,
Elizabethan Stage (Oxford, 1923), ii. 261–5; Lea, i. 42–7, ii. 398, 648 ff., 658 ff.

only adequate means of expression.[1] As an older man, crucially posed at the crossways of life, with a boy on one hand and a fool on the other, he compares as well with the *mago* as the *capitano*, the mask that Shakespeare adapts in creating Prospero. The point is not that Armado resembles Prospero any more than *Love's Labour's Lost* resembles *The Tempest*, but that he is integral in ways that Berowne is not.

The limits of Shakespeare's pastoral tone here are mockery and melancholy: the 'man replete with mocks' (v. ii. 839) and the man who has 'seen the day of wrong' (v. ii. 720). And it is the latter who has the last word. If one reads the play as a comedy of manners, then Berowne has the best of what conflict of character there is and, under analysis, the plot goes to pieces. Read as a pastoral, it comes together; with Armado as the other term in a comic dialectic of the mercurial with the saturnine: *allegro* with *penseroso*.

Melancholy, the humour of contemplation, belongs as much to the scholar's mental landscape as to the lover's:

The Florentine Neo-Platonists . . . discovered that Plotinus and his followers had thought as highly of Saturn as Aristotle had thought of melancholy. . . . He symbolized the 'Mind' of the world where Jupiter merely symbolized its 'Soul'; he had thought out what Jupiter had merely learned to govern; he stood, in short, for profound contemplation as opposed to mere practical action. . . . They hailed him as their celestial patron just as they reconciled themselves to melancholy as their terrestrial condition. The most illustrious members of the Florentine circle . . . referred to themselves, only half playfully, as 'Saturnians', and they discovered to their immense satisfaction that Plato, too, had been born under the sign of Saturn.[2]

The unity of Shakespeare's first scene, Ferdinand's academy, with his second, Armado and Moth in a landscape ('besieged with sable-coloured melancholy'), is that of Saturn. And so, mythologically speaking, is the unity of the hermetic *protasis* with the erotic *epitasis*. Study and love both issue in melancholy, a 'contem-

[1] *Platonische Renaissance*, p. 122. Cf. A. Harbage, '*Love's Labour's Lost* and the Early Shakespeare', *Philological Quarterly*, xli (1962), 29.

[2] E. Panofsky, *Life and Art of Albrecht Dürer* (Princeton, 1955), p. 167.

plative absorption in the idea of mortality'.[1] This comes to its climax in the catastrophe with the news of the French King's death. As anyone who saw the Stratford production of 1946 knows, this most conventional of pastoral devices makes a notable *coup de théâtre*, a perfect turn on the old motif of death's presence even among the nymphs and shepherds:

> Worthies, away! The scene begins to cloud. (v. ii. 718)

Marcade's entry mars Arcadia. One may deplore our Poet's conceit, but in the light of all the Nashe-Harvey-Marprelate punning it hardly looks unconscious.

Armado is the only figure who, thanks to his time of life, passes for good and all, like the play's verbal initiative, from the brightness of spring and summer into the shadow of autumn and winter. At this point the motif that serves to compose the plot around him is the Ages of Man. All seven (as Jacques computes them) can be found in Act V if one counts Moth as both schoolboy and infant Hercules. Certainly the cardinal four are there, corresponding to the humours and the seasons, with Death calling the tune:

> King: Now, at the latest minute of the hour,
>   Grant us your loves.
> Princess: A time methinks too short
>   To make a world-without-end bargain in:
>   No no, my lord, your grace is perjured much.
>   (v. ii. 783-6)

This refusal, followed by the *dulce amarum* of Armado's final travesty of a Platonic dialogue, solemnizes the marriage of mockery to melancholy. In a world of Marcade's making, the eclogue of cuckoo and owl is all the masque of Hymen there is.

Armado may lack the wit of Berowne but, as his finale reveals, he knows the language of the mysteries. The voice of all the gods is not mute for him as for Berowne. When the last image, as well as the last word, turns out to be his, 'Monsieur Melancholy' has

[1] E. Panofsky, *Meaning in the Visual Arts* (New York, 1955), p. 313.

outfaced 'Signior Love', however sorrily, as lover, as heroic soul, and as Orphic sage.[1]

The commentaries usually say that in the songs Shakespeare endorses 'nature' or the 'going-on power of life', as against courtly artificiality.[2] But if a study of pastoralism can do anything, it can correct the view that for the Renaissance artist nature and art are merely opposites. They are rather the opposites which he undertakes to reconcile by imposing the unity of an art that goes beyond art. In the songs of cuckoo and owl, the 'tenuous alliance between dialectics and pastoral', as it has been called, can be seen at its most tenuous.[3]

The debates of the birds have been an artifice of pastoral poetry at least since Hesiod.[4] And with all their spontaneous rustic charm Shakespeare's cuckoo and owl carry comic implications of the cryptic. This is, as usual, a matter of allusion and context. Taken together they hint at two notorious enigmas of poetic theology, Bacchus-Apollo and Mercury-Minerva, both signifying the wisdom of folly.

In grasping the 'theology' of the cuckoo song, one is helped by a poem of Chaucer's in the *Canterbury Tales*, the little-loved fable of Phoebus Apollo and the talking crow. This is a sort of riddle in the *pourquoi* tradition, telling how crows which were once white come to be black; the reason being that a crow once told Apollo of his wife's infidelity and was thus rewarded by the ungrateful god. Like so many of the myths in which the pagan mysteries inhere, this one comes down to Chaucer and the Renaissance by way of Ovid and the medieval *Ovide moralisé*.[5]

Chaucer puts this mocking and melancholy piece of love psychology into the mouth of the gentle but sardonic Manciple, together with one of his rare allusions to Plato:

---

[1] Cf. *As You Like It*, III. ii. 251; R. Poggioli, 'The Pastoral of the Self', *Daedalus*, lxxxviii (1959), 686.

[2] J. Palmer, *Comic Characters of Shakespeare* (London, 1946), p. 5; C. L. Barber, *Shakespeare's Festive Comedy* (Princeton, 1959), p. 118. Cf. J. A. K. Thomson, *Shakespeare and the Classics* (London, 1952), p. 76.   [3] Wind, *Pagan Mysteries*, p. 99.

[4] J. H. Hanford, 'Classical Eclogue and Medieval Debate', *Romanic Review*, ii (1911), 16–31, 129–43.

[5] Seznec, Ch. III. Cf. Ovid, *Metamorphoses*, ii. 542 ff. (Apollo and Coronis).

The wise Plato seith, as ye may rede,
The word moot nede accorde with the dede.
If men shal telle proprely a thyng,
The word moot cosyn be to the werkyng.
(IX. 207–10, ed. F. Robinson)

And the moral the Manciple draws from it, sententiously and at
great length, is directed against the talkative crow—and against
himself for having reproved one of his fellow pilgrims, the drunken
cook, and so made an enemy:

A jangler is to God abhomynable. (l. 343)

But since the crow in the fable, like the Manciple, speaks the truth,
little as Apollo and the Cook like to hear it, one may draw another
moral altogether—the moral of *Love's Labour's Lost*.

The word that Chaucer's bird sings to Apollo is the same one that
Shakespeare's sings to Ferdinand and his court:

This crowe sang 'Cokkow! Cokkow! Cokkow!' (l. 243)

> Cuckoo, cuckoo: O word of fear,
> Unpleasing to a married ear! (v. ii. 967–8)

And while the lords and ladies may think of Armado, their audience
may think of them. Apollo without Bacchus never won and kept
fair lady.

In view of the occasion for a hint of *discordia concors* in the *Manciple's Tale*, as in *Love's Labour's Lost*, it is notable that Chaucer does
introduce his fable with an invocation to Bacchus, prompted by the
Cook's drunkenness:

> O thou Bacus, yblessed be thy name,
> That so kanst turnen ernest into game!
> Worshipe and thank be to thy deitee!
> Of that mateere ye gete namoore of me.
> Telle on thy tale, Manciple, I thee preye. (ll. 99–103)

Whatever this means concerning Chaucer and hermeneutics, here
is a prime motif of poetic theology in transition from Ovid to
Shakespeare. But might there not well be more to the Manciple's
tale than has met the ear of 'an heep of lerned men'?

The owl song which answers the cuckoo brings to mind the Hermathena, symbol of more than one academy. When the Bolognese adopted it from Cicero's *Tusculanum* it was understood to paraphrase *festina lente* in the emblematic language of the mysteries: 'the swiftness of the god of eloquence [combined] with the steadfastness of the goddess of wisdom.'[1] Because all the divine names imply their contraries, it also stands for the hermetic eloquence of silence (Pan's *ite* in the *Aminta*) and the palladian wisdom of folly: an apt device for the end of an academic comedy. The practice of such wisdom means speaking in riddles or parables, as every professor should know.

The songs composed by pedant and hedge-priest for Armado's finale are thus both learned and ludicrous in the most ancient and approved manner. The words of Mercury, conductor of souls, may be harsh, as that enigmatic voice at the end of the Quarto text affirms, but they are as much a rite of art as the songs of Apollo; and the word 'moot nede accorde with the dede'.

> You that way: we this way.[2]

With the foolish wisdom of his melancholy union with Jaquenetta, Armado has at least propitiated both patrons of Hercules and all three of Paris in the way that Bruno recommends.[3]

> But 'twas beyond a mortal's share
> To wander solitary there.
> (Marvell, *The Garden*, ll. 61–2)

The comic fall of Berowne, Ferdinand, and company has, by comparison, a faint echo of Ficino on the loss of academic Eden:

In the gardens of Academe poets would listen beneath the laurels to Apollo singing. In the courtyard orators would consider Mercury

---

[1] Wind, *Pagan Mysteries*, pp. 166–7. Cf. Duchemin, i. 19 ff., on Hermes as pastoral rival of Apollo and predecessor of Dionysos.

[2] Folio exeunt, omitted by New Cambridge editors. Cf. Horace, *Odes*, I. x. 17 (Hymn to Mercury): 'Tu pias laetis animas reponis': Thou dost conduct pious souls to the happy [places].

[3] Bruno, ii. 417 (*De gli eroici furori*). Cf. iii. 1 (*Candelaio*): 'Academico di nulla academia, detto il fastidito . . . "In tristitia hilaris, in hilaritate tristis" ': Academic of no academy, called the Fastidious . . . 'In sadness mirthful, in mirth sad'. Also Touchstone and Audrey, *As You Like It*, V. iv. 52 ff.

declaiming. In the arcade (porticu) . . . jurists would overhear Jove himself ratifying laws. . . . . And in the inmost places of the temple (penetralibus) philosophers would recollect (agnoscent) with Saturn his divine knowledge of the secret contemplative mind (coelestium arcanorum contemplatorum). . . .

But how often in fact does Philosophy stray out of the gardens of Academe, not only losing its salves (unguenta) and its flowers but even—oh most abominable! (proh nefas)—falling among thieves and lost priests. There she wanders about hither and yon, denuded of all her dignified and lovely attributes (gravitatis insignibus) and, as it were, profane; and so much so that she appears deformed and pleases neither Phoebus on the one hand nor Mercury on the other, her two familiar gods (familiaribus); nor, what is more, does she recommend herself (probetur) to Jove or mother Minerva.[1]

From the beginning of the *Commentaria Platonis* to the end of *Love's Labour's Lost* is not as far as one expects, thanks to the quicksilver language of pastoral.

Shakespeare does not invoke the mysteries with quite the rapture of his continental predecessors. And the magic of his phrasing in 'When daisies pied and violets blue' and 'When icicles hang by the wall' is not explained by pointing out that they are consciously, if mockingly, Orphic. But poetic theology enters as deeply into the sense and structure of his comic theatre as into Tasso's.

One may say that he cultivates the mysteries or laughs at them, mocks Ralegh in the mask of Armado or praises him. *Serio ludere* ensures that like Cervantes he will always have the advantage of his interlocutor. Is Don Quixote the fool or the hero of his creator? The best answer to this is an essay on pastoral travesty of the heroic style at the turn of the century.[2]

The virtue of *Love's Labour's Lost* is stylistic; a language combining mystery with wit to the exclusion of the sentimental. The whole play, says Granville-Barker, 'demands style'.[3] What should one understand by this? It must mean the right degree of self-consciousness in all the actions of life, especially language. From

---

[1] Ficino, ii. 1129–30 (Proemium ad Laurentium).
[2] E. Auerbach, *Mimesis* (Bern, 1946), Ch. XIV.
[3] Granville-Barker, ii. 423.

such self-consciousness, mystery as well as wit results, for only the way an action is performed shows that the actor knows what he is doing. The stylist thus sets up as his own best critic.

To like *Love's Labour's Lost* one has to be something of a dandy. Though it improves enormously on Lyly and Peele, no one has ever thought it a great comedy. How it comes to stand higher in the repertory than, say, *Epicoene*, is another melancholy mystery. Like the *Two Gentlemen*, it is one of those inferior early works in which a great comedian gives away his predilections. And a pastoral reading will reverse no one's judgement on it, only show it for what it is. The comedy in which Shakespeare fully realizes his early pastoral style is not this one, but *A Midsummer-Night's Dream*.

6

A MIDSUMMER-NIGHT'S DREAM: BOTTOM TRANSLATED

> Had the cult of the incongruous produced nothing but
> monsters, it would have only a limited, anthropological
> interest.   WIND

(i) *The Voice of Integrity*

WHAT any reader—any passer-by at the Folger—knows about
A Midsummer-Night's Dream is right enough. At the centre of the
play there is a memorable vision of the Fairy Queen enamoured of a
monster, a man with the head of an ass. And in another connection
Puck says,

> Lord, what fools these mortals be! (III. ii. 115)

All that the professional reader does is explain if and why Shakespeare's elaboration on this mythology and these words satisfies
him. So there are the aesthetic readers like Chambers and De la
Mare, and the ethical or doctrinal ones like Paul Olson, with
numerous compromises between.[1] What an account of Shakespeare's
pastoralism may do is confirm the first of these by encouraging the
mythological reading of a play that no one would deny is mythological.[2]

In the light of the *Aminta* this most mature of the early comedies
displays a familiar combination of poetic theology and *serio ludere*:
the love fables of an Ovid or a Chaucer accommodated to the 'ludic

---

[1] Chambers, *Shakespeare: A Survey*, Ch. IX; W. De la Mare, *Pleasures and Speculations*
(London, 1940), pp. 270–305; P. Olson, '*A Midsummer-Night's Dream* and the
Meaning of Court Marriage', *ELH*, xxiv (1957), 95–119.

[2] C. S. Baldwin and D. L. Clarke, *Renaissance Literary Theory and Practice* (New
York, 1939), pp. 146–54.

genius' of Tasso's later English contemporary.[1] The mysteries supposed to be inherent in such fables are once again playfully rehearsed for the sake of all that the cult of language stood for in the London of the 1590s.

As in the *Two Gentlemen*, Euphuistic versions of the courtier and his lady are merged with figures from mythology in a celebration of the powers of love and poetry; only in this instance some of the immortals and demigods whom the young lovers prefigure stand among the dramatis personae in their own right. A fuller chain of being than in any other early comedy reaches from hempen homespun to fairy gossamer, and as in all such Platonizing mythopoeia these extremes meet. The marriage of Theseus and Hippolyta frames a quartet of more impassioned love votaries, who in turn envision a 'more remov'd mystery' of Bottom and Titania. And by virtue of the pseudo-Orphic unction of Shakespeare's style, a pastoral theocracy of Diana, Venus, and Cupid, Apollo and Bacchus, Hercules and Orpheus invisibly impends.

As in *Love's Labour's Lost*, the heroic mode is at once conceitedly passed over in favour of the inner life of the lover. Theseus announces his wedding day and with it the pastoral scope of the play:

> Hippolyta, I wooed thee with my sword,
> And won thy love doing thee injuries:
> But I will wed thee in another key,
> With pomp, with triumph, and with revelling.
>
> (I. i. 16–19)

A Herculean note, proper to epithalamic *Kômos* and a kinsman of the god, sounds here. Militant chastity is to be reconciled in due ceremony with the pleasure of love.

But in an audience mindful of the conventions some doubt must arise about the fitness of Theseus for this office. His opening complaint about the moon, although meant as a compliment to Hippolyta, jars if one listens to it carefully:

> . . . but O, methinks how slow
> This old moon wanes! She lingers my desires,

---

[1] J. Huizinga, *Homo Ludens*, trans. anon. (Boston, 1955), p. 181.

> Like to a step-dame, or a dowager,
> Long withering out a young man's revenue.
>
> (I. i. 3–6)

So unflattering a reference to the deity in whom the triad Diana-Luna-Hecate is enfolded hints at something less fitting than a lover's impatience with chastity—some failure of the proper mythic humour.[1]

It compares unfavourably with Hippolyta's graceful and compliant response:

> Four days will quickly steep themselves in night:
> Four nights will quickly dream away the time:
> And then the moon, like to a silver bow
> New-bent in heaven, shall behold the night
> Of our solemnities. (I. i. 7–11)

Nothing Theseus says in the entire scene, whether about divinest melancholy (I. i. 14) or about chastity (I. i. 65 ff.) suggests that his is the voice of integrity. But this fluent and mysterious speech of Hippolyta's, prophesying a rite of Venus in which Diana will comply, is wholly in tune with Shakespeare's own metamorphic unfolding of plot and image.

Pat upon the hero's boast of being fluent in the other key of pastoral comes the petition of Egeus against his daughter Hermia. It falls predictably across the scene of love, like an *Et in Arcadia ego*, putting Theseus to a choice between virtue and pleasure reminiscent of that of Hercules or Paris. His judgement confirms the ascendancy at this point of the goddess Chastity:

> Or else to wed Demetrius as he would,
> Or on Diana's altar to protest
> For aye austerity and single life. (I. i. 88–90)

No shepherd-prince apt for reconciliation would impose on Hermia and Lysander a preference for virtue or chastity exclusive of pleasure. And while Theseus tries solemnly to impose law on love and to

---

[1] Cf. A. Fraunce, *Amintas Dale*, sigs. L–M; *Orphica*, pp. 58–9 (Hymns to Hecate, to Prothyraea). In *Love's Labour's Lost* (IV. ii. 36–8) Hecate, the 'presiding spirit wherever three roads meet', is comically invoked as Dictynna; cf. Thomson, *Shakespeare and the Classics*, pp. 69, 114.

rule his subjects by division, his more imaginative consort-to-be listens in evident dismay:

> Come, Hippolyta: what cheer, my love? (I. i. 122)

The mood, as one might expect of Elizabethan fairy poetry, is mildly mock-heroic, but not satiric. It is the Platonizing mood of facetious compliment that one finds in Bellini's *Feast of the Gods*:

> In fact, the whole play is a bantering game in which all parties are quizzed in turn, and which, at the same time, makes game of the audience as well.[1]

It is the young lovers, Lysander and Hermia, who assume the state of mind proper to the rite of Venus and Diana that Theseus announces. Crossed by the *geron*, provoked by Demetrius, their Proteus figure, they move into a rapture as wise in its folly as the wisdom of Theseus is foolish:

> The course of true love never did run smooth . . .
> And in the wood, a league without the town . . .
> There will I stay for thee. (I. i. 134–68)

> I swear to thee by Cupid's strongest bow . . .
> By the simplicity of Venus' doves,
> By that which knitteth souls and prospers loves,
> And by that fire which burned the Carthage queen
> When the false Troyan under sail was seen,
> By all the vows that ever men have broke . . .
> Tomorrow truly will I meet with thee. (I. i. 169–78)

In pastoral, Aeneas is the false Trojan, and dying in the flames of love the more than reasonable way to live.

More clearly than Hermia, Helena, a Julia complaining of her Proteus, now echoes the mystical phrasing of a Ficino or a Castiglione on Amor:[2]

---

[1] H. H. Furness, ed., *Variorum Shakespeare* (Philadelphia, 1895), x. 325. Also cited in De la Mare, p. 296.

[2] Ficino, ii. 1344 (*In Convivium*): 'Per has animi acies saepenumero incitatur ad universales rerum ideas, quas in se continet intenduas': Through these [images], the eyes of the soul are awaked to behold the universal ideas of things which the soul holds within itself (trans. S. R. Jayne). B. Castiglione, *Il libro del cortegiano*, ed. V. Cian (Florence, 1947), p. 494: 'bellezza . . . che si vede con gli occhi della mente'. Hoby translates verbatim: 'beauty that is seen with the eyes of the mind'.

Things base and vile, holding no quantity,
Love can transpose to form and dignity.
Love looks not with the eyes, but with the mind:
And therefore is winged Cupid painted blind.
Nor hath Love's mind of any judgement taste:
Wings and no eyes figure unheedy haste.
And therefore is Love said to be a child:
Because in choice he is so oft beguiled. (I. i. 232–9)

The opening movement of the play, *emanatio*, is thus made an explicit rehearsal of the blind love theme from the *Two Gentlemen*, with Shakespeare inviting his audience to sit, not in judgement on folly, but in conscious aesthetic delight at the turning of it into wisdom.

The point is that he composes, not as a high priest of Neo-Platonism, but as a love poet. But nor does his plot teach the young lovers, these Bacchoi with their 'crazed title', that love is *not* 'short as any dream':

. . . momentany as a sound,
Swift as a shadow, short as any dream,
Brief as the lightning in the collied night,
That, in a spleen, unfolds both heaven and earth.
(I. i. 143–6)

On the contrary, his very unfolding of the plot, the mysterious change and flow of his pastoral myth and language itself makes a dazzling exhibition of volatility—the one Orphic voice wholly divisible into many.

This is seen to advantage in the major transition of the first act, from the lovers taking flight to the forest to the clownish craftsmen preparing their play. The theme shifts in familiar Shakespearian fashion from the mock-heroic praise of love to the mock pastoral praise of poetry. Bottom and his fellow Thespians act out an analogue of the previous scene which is at once a travesty and a truer echo of integrity.

Like Theseus, Bottom proclaims himself a whole man, as apt for Pyramus as Hercules. But when the play decided on is the passion of the lover, he and his fellows enter into the spirit of Ovid's fable with a foolish reverence proper to the mysterious wisdom it veils. Pyramus or Thisbe, Bacchic lion or Venus' doves, all is one to Bottom, the pan-erotic man wise enough to play his part over the full range between 'most obscenely, and courageously' (I. ii. 100). Theseus in his speech on fabling in the last act shows no such ludicrous piety. But the tendency of the plot is none the less to ring a change on the union of contraries, impatience and compliance, which he and Hippolyta at first represent. In the end Theseus, like Diana, comes to comply.

Bottom's scenes mark one of the extremities of Shakespeare's pastoral range of style, and of his evocation of the Bacchic. His interest here, as throughout, beyond that of making fun out of clownishness, is like Ovid's in his love poetry: an interest in what one student of the mythologies calls 'les possibilités d'une langue évoluée, apte à tout dire, à tout suggérer'.[1]

(ii) *Bacchus-Apollo*

If *A Midsummer-Night's Dream* is a wedding play of Diana reconciled to Venus, as in Spenser (*Faerie Queene*, III. vi. 25), then the critical question is how such reconciliation is brought about.[2] What does it mean to an audience always in its senses to say that out of 'enforced chastity' (III. i. 191) is brought pleasure, 'the Venus of the sky' (III. ii. 107)? It suggests that Shakespeare's resources are poetic theology and *serio ludere*: pastoral mythology and pastoral style. But how exactly do these work for him?

The action of his mythologizing—as of Ovid's—is metamorphic: transfiguration; the power to change things in man, nature, and the divine. And the agent of this change is at first said to be Cupid, who is invoked in the famous speech on the love-shaft, the Vestal,

---

[1] E. de Saint-Denis, 'Le Malicieux Ovide', in *Ovidiana*, ed. N. I. Herescu (Paris, 1958), p. 200. For the rivalry of Theseus and Bacchus over Ariadne, and the erotic alliance of Bacchus and Venus, cf. ibid. For Shakespeare's knowledge of Ovid, cf. Bullough, i. 161.

[2] Cf. *Faerie Queene*, IV, proem, 4. This is, of course, the mythological sense of the *Aminta*. In *Love's Labour's Lost* it is reversed. For the emblematic form of Venus-Diana or Venus-Virgo (*Aeneid*, i. 315), cf. *Shepheardes Calender*, April, emblem; Wind, *Pagan Mysteries*, pp. 73–5.

and Love-in-idleness (II. i. 148 ff.). In this version of the *Castitas-Amor-Voluptas* Oberon and Puck are evidently masks of Cupid, the one showing his mighty lordship, the other his childish mischief. His is the power which, through the love-juice, induces both the passion of Titania for Bottom and the nocturnal round of changes in the young lovers. These last, though somewhat over-indulged, make a more expressive parable of the inspired reason of love-madness than the *Two Gentlemen*.

The first of Shakespeare's means of bringing reconciliation about is thus simply calling on the love god by name, or making a classical allusion—he allows for both understandings. But there turns out to be more to the process than the mere invocation of Cupid—over whose flower Love-in-idleness 'Diana's Bud' will in any case prevail (IV. i. 72). In this herbal symbolism, which more than one reader has thought the germ of the plot, Shakespeare draws on a fund of Ovidian pastoral lore which he shares with Montemayor and Tasso, among others.[1] And as might be expected, such symbolism carries with it—indeed, requires—a whole context of mythology and ritual proper to its mode.

If *emanatio* is to give place to *raptio* and finally to *remeatio*, then other Olympians than Cupid will be involved:

> And, when Love speaks, the voice of all the gods
> Make heaven drowsy with the harmony.
>
> (*LLL*, IV. iii. 341–2)

The god of ritual mystery and poetic drama, through whose power of *raptio* a theocrasy of Venus and Diana may finally be reached, is not Cupid but Bacchus.

The prevalence of the moon in Shakespeare's conception of this action has often been remarked on. And in the lunar sphere, as Ficino explains, poetic theology calls the gnostic power in the heavens Bacchus and the vivifying power in souls on earth Thalia.

---

[1] Ovid, *Remedia Amoris*, l. 139; Montemayor, *Diana*, i (Selvaggio's story); Tasso, *Aminta*, II. ii. 270: 'E ne l'ozio l'amor sempre germoglia': And love always buds in idleness. Cf. R. Tobler, 'Shakespeares *Sommernachtstraum* und Montemayors *Diana*', *Shakespeare Jahrbuch*, xxxiv (1898), 358–66; E. Schanzer, 'The Central Theme of *A Midsummer-Night's Dream*', *University of Toronto Quarterly*, xx (1951), 233–8. In the *Diana* the love-juice is supplied by Lady Felicia who dwells in the temple of Diana.

As in the Orphic hymns which Ficino has in mind, Bacchus is here the Winnower (*Liknitus*). And Thalia is both one of the Graces and the Muse who wears the mask of comedy and the ivy wreath, and carries the shepherd's staff of pastoral.[1]

Now I take it to be part of the mock-esoteric delight of this comedy of night and magic that Bacchus, the chief actor, is never named. His presence as the god of darkness is hinted at through his attributes or else implied, on the governing principle of *discordia concors*, by the invocation of Apollo. While Puck, with the swiftness of Cupid, puts a girdle round the earth for Love-in-idleness, this invocation is spoken by Helena to her Proteus:

> Run when you will: the story shall be changed:
> Apollo flies, and Daphne holds the chase;
> The dove pursues the griffin; the mild hind
> Makes speed to catch the tiger . . . , (II. i. 230–3)

a speech full of emblems signifying the union of apparent contraries by way of inversion.

At this point in the play's mythological argument the ascendancy of Diana is transposed into the ascendancy of Apollo and so, by inversion, into that of Bacchus. In sacred rites, says Macrobius, it is a religious observance of the mystery for the sun to be called Apollo by day but to be thought of as Bacchus by night.[2] And Bacchus it is who dominates the central nocturnal scenes of the fairy plot in which Oberon and Titania are the first to act out that turning of chastity into pleasure, division into union, which is the dramatic action.

Any attempt to put the mythic as distinct from verbal sense of such language into plain words is likely to be unsatisfactory. And any modern audience will have reservations about a dramatic

---

[1] Ficino, i. 131 (*Theologia Platonica*); cf. *Orphica*, p. 83 (Hymn to Liknitus Bacchus); Taylor, *Mystical Hymns of Orpheus*, p. 26 n. (Hymn to the Moon). In the *Republic* (ii. 364E), the Orphica is called 'offspring of the Moon and the Muses'.

[2] Macrobius, *Saturnalia*, I. xviii. 8: 'In sacris enim haec religiosi arcani observatio tenetur, ut sol, cum in supero id est, in diurno hemisphaerio est, Apollo vocitetur: cum in infero, id est nocturno, Dionysus, qui est Liber pater, habeatur.' The parallelism of *vocitetur* and *habeatur* suggests that, as in *A Midsummer-Night's Dream*, Apollo may be named but Bacchus only held in mind.

poetry which begins by covertly assuming whatever it sets out to perform. 'Each of the gods [of the Greek theology] is in all, and all are in each.'[1] If the truth is that Diana and Venus, like Apollo and Bacchus, are one, why all the palaver?

Art, one may say in answer, like nature, yields nothing without ceremonies. And here it is Shakespeare's pleasure to play on the modality of pastoral language with all the imagistic skill and sophistication of a Mantegna or a Titian.

The names and attributes of Oberon and Titania suggest in the omni-allusive manner of mythology both the discord and the concord which the fairy plot enacts. Oberon means chastity, temperance, heroic severity, as in Spenser's *Faerie Queene*, where he and Huon of Bordeaux are the patrons of Sir Guyon (II. i. 6). But he also serves Cupid, consort of the more wanton of the play's two presiding goddesses; and Titania jealously imputes an almost Jovial wantonness to him. Yet in the same speech, in an easy transition from elfin to Arcadian, she envisages him as an Apolline shepherd:

> And in the shape of Corin sat all day,
> Playing on pipes of corn, and versing love,
> To amorous Phillida. (II. i. 66–8)

Titania herself similarly suggests, by her name, the chastity of the play's other presiding goddess, as in the *Metamorphoses* (iii. 173). Yet to Oberon she is 'proud'—eager for the male, glosses Johnson— and a 'rash wanton' (II. i. 60–3). And a good case can be made for taking the implied tenor of her relations with the changeling and with Bottom to be Bacchic.[2]

---

[1] Taylor, *Mystical Hymns of Orpheus*, pp. xxvii–xxviii.

[2] Cf. D. C. Miller, 'Titania and the Changeling', *English Studies*, xxii (1940), 66–70. Titania is a term of the Platonic cosmology, not for the moon but the stars: cf. Ficino, i. 614 (*Epistolae*): 'Nam mundi totius animum saepenumero Jovem Platonici nuncupant, qui coelum ac terras, camposque liquentes, lucentemque globum Lunae, Titaniaque astra intus alit, totamque infusus per artus agitat molem, et magno se corpore miscet': For the Platonists often call Jove the soul of all the world, who inwardly sustains heaven and the regions of earth, and the flowing expanse of the sea, and the shining sphere of Luna, and the Titanian stars, and (infused by magic) he moves the whole mass, and mingles himself with the great body of things.

The quarrel of the fairy king and queen over

A lovely boy, stol'n from an Indian King (II. i. 22)

echoes the Olympian quarrel in the *Metamorphoses* over Semele's infant son, as well as the jealousy of Apollo over Coronis and the Thessalian youth. And Shakespeare's unseen changeling boy, with his loveliness, and his attachment to women, and his Indian past, is no less reminiscent of one aspect of 'dainty Bacchus' than Bottom, with his ass's head and ecstasy, is of another. Oberon and Puck maliciously substitute one of these for the other; and Titania garlands both like Bacchus and makes them all her joy, giving Bottom the very roses of Venus mentioned in the *Ars Amatoria* (l. 232) and elsewhere.[1]

To an audience familiar with Ovidian mythology and how the Platonists read it, the esoteric sense of the fairy plot is quite as overt as its absurdity.[2] Much as the first act travesties the Platonistic warrior-lover, the third act travesties the lover-angel. As in the rape of Ariadne, the agent of transcendence and transfiguration is Bacchus inspiration of the lover and ally of Venus. And in Titania's love for Bottom, in spite of the comedy, a Bacchic mystery is to be discerned. It relates to those mysteries of Orpheus and Marsyas which Tasso rehearses in the *Aminta*, this time by way of the fable of Midas.

Midas, says Ovid, had once been instructed in the Bacchic mysteries by Orpheus himself. And when he was in the pseudo-Orphic predicament of having to judge between Apollo and Marsyas as musicians, he preferred the music of the satyr, Marsyas —or Pan as Hyginus, Cooper, and Lyly all call him. Bacchus being at that time in India, Midas was rewarded by Apollo with the ass's ears: 'Quale cor in iudicando habuisti, tales et auriculas habebis':

Midas: What hast thou done Apollo? the eares of an Asse upon the head of a king?

---

[1] Cf. Ovid, *Metamorphoses*, iii. 29–iv.2; *Orphica*, p. 83 (Hymn to Liknitus): '[Bacchus] ... of Nymphs the blossom bright, / And of fair Venus, Goddess of delight' (trans. Taylor).

[2] Cf. C. B. Cooper, *Some Elizabethan Opinions of the Poetry and Character of Ovid* (Menasha, 1914); J. McLennen, *On the Meaning and Function of Allegory in the English Renaissance* (Ann Arbor, 1947).

Apollo: And well worthie, when the dulness of an Asse is in the eares
of a king. (*Midas*, IV. i. 141-4)

Lyly's version, cited here after Hyginus', is one that Shakespeare is
likely to have known.[1]

The Midas fable evidently concerns the hearing of a divine
harmony, Apolline as well as Bacchic; the finding of the One in the
Many. It is a riddle about a mystery, not a comedy of character.
Cooper's *Thesaurus*, the supposed source of Shakespeare's mythography, moralizes it as a lesson about a tyrant and his informers.
But Shakespeare seems to understand it aesthetically, as an allegory of intellectual love. In the best manner of the Platonic theorists
he has Bottom sing, and love comes in the ears of Titania:

> I pray thee, gentle mortal, sing again!
> Mine ear is much enamoured of thy note . . .
> So is mine eye enthralled to thy shape. . . . (III. i. 130-2)

And later, with more than a hint of Midas, Bottom brays about
needing to go to the barber and having a good ear for 'the tongs
and bones' (IV. i. 23-9).

Editors do not make much of this phrase beyond the obvious
reference to primitive music, and nor does the *Oxford English
Dictionary*. But one of the patristic mythographers reprinted during
the sixteenth century offers a clue in his interpretation of the
judgement of Midas. This mystic fable, says Fulgentius, refers to
the origin of music, as Orpheus and Hermes Trismegistus have
written; and the origin of music is threefold: The singing voice
(*cantatium*), the striking of strings (*citharizantium*), and the blowing
of a pipe (*tibicinatium*).[2] This account is standard for the classics,
the strings being Apollo's and the pipe being attributed to Bacchus,
as in the *Aeneid*:

> aut ubi curva choros indixit tibia Bacchi.[3] (xi. 737)

---

[1] Ovid, *Metamorphoses*, xi. 92; M. Justinus, *Historiarum Philippicarum*, trans. A.
Golding (London, 1570), sig. H₅ᵛ; Hyginus, *Fabularum Liber*, ed. J. Micyllus (Basle,
1549), p. 45; T. Cooper, *Thesaurus Linguae Romanae et Brittanicae* (London, 1573),
cited in Bullough, i. 397-8; J. Lyly, *Works*, ed. R. W. Bond (Oxford, 1902), iii. 143
(*Midas*).

[2] Fulgentius, *Mythologiarum Libri III*, in Hyginus, pp. 145-6.

[3] Or where the curved flute proclaims the Bacchic dance (Loeb trans.).

So when Bottom calls for 'the tongs and bones' after ravishing Titania's ear with his singing voice, what is hinted at may be some burlesque version of the *cithara*, which is struck with a plectrum, and the *tibia* or *fistula*, which is of bone: one more serio-comic allusion to the Orphic harmony of the whole man, this time in terms not of acting but music.

For by this point in the play Bottom is in fact all an audience's joy, as well as all Titania's. Yet could one say that since Hazlitt the supposition has not crept in that with Bottom, as with Armado and Falstaff, Shakespeare somehow wrought better than he knew? Or, at least, that he did so at the expense of that side of his genius which delighted in mythologizing, pastoralizing, Euphuism, and conceits—all the humanistic vices of his day?

In both of Bottom's scenes with Titania there is allusion to Midas, not only verbally, but by means of the ass's head as well. This Midas-figure is nobody's fool but Shakespeare's own: he wears not the ears only as in the *Metamorphoses*, which Lyly follows, nor the whole body as in the *Golden Ass* or in Lucian, but the head. Shakespeare is the more himself for never quite being the Platonizing humanist he could be. Yet the 'ass's noll' still carries suggestions of a Bacchic rite of self-transcendence through humility, as in Ovid and Apuleius, or in the *Praise of Folly*. There Folly begins mockingly by comparing herself and her audience to Pan and Midas in the fable, and ends in a notable Erasmian *serio ludere* by invoking Silenus, Socrates, and Jesus, too, all patrons of the ass. Bottom, like Folly, can put on the language of 1 Corinthians.

Encomia of the ass as 'both absurd in essence and the carrier of divine mysteries' were too well known by the 1590s to escape implication in such scenes as these of Bottom and the Fairy Queen.[1] And like every other figure in the play, Bottom translated means reverence as well as laughter, mystery as well as humour, wisdom as well as folly.

But what is important to notice is not so much the esoteric in its own right as Shakespeare's lightness in touching on it. As in *Love's Labour's Lost*, his humour is such that a paragon of integrity like

---

[1] K. W. Scoular, *Natural Magic* (Oxford, 1965), p. 112.

Bottom is none the less so for being travestied. The humorous reversal of the appearance of things works in the interest, not of satire, but of an otherworldliness proper to pastoral. This is his version of those *facetiae* which typify the mode from the *Phaedrus* and *Bucolics* onwards. The scene in which Oberon witnesses his Diana-figure in the dark god's embrace achieves a pitch of low comedy and high mystery combined that must be as notable an instance of *serio ludere* as Renaissance pastoral can show. Here if anywhere love psychology, mythological rite, and comic drama coincide in a single satisfying mode of imaging.

Oberon and Puck do not cease to regard this union of contraries as hateful fantasy and folly. But an Apolline odium for Bacchic orgies is, in context, something very different from the mere moralizing of fables found in Cooper, or Fraunce, or some modern makers of Shakespeare sermons. The Titania who says

O, how mine eyes do loathe his visage now! (IV. i. 78)

is hardly reading a lesson in conjugal obedience. This, like Puck's

Lord, what fools these mortals be! (III. ii. 115)

is the language, not of doctrine, but of pastoral-comical enigma. And in this mode, as one knows from the *Orfeo*, there is no one right point of view on what is enacted but the audience's, which is always in its senses and knows that every fable veils a mystery. Even the Apollo-Marsyas contest is a riddle that Midas perhaps knew, having been initiated into the mysteries by Orpheus, but would not divulge.

Pastoralism is nowhere more evidently Shakespeare's model than in the two set pieces which open and close the central movement of *raptio*: Titania on the discord in nature caused by her quarrel with Oberon (II. i. 81 ff.) and Theseus and Hippolyta on the concord of their Spartan hounds (IV. i. 102 ff.), an echo of Sidney's *Arcadia* (I. x). Though worked right into the plot, these are the counterparts of the *intermedi* of Proteus and Pan in the *Aminta*; ritual invocations, full of allusion, by which the bringing of harmony ('one mutual cry') out of 'our debate . . . our dissension' is formally announced.

How Shakespeare reconciles Diana and Venus, one may now say, is in the manner of Tasso in his *intermedi*. First he poses a Protean discord in which Diana prevails. Then he transposes it, by way of Apollo-Bacchus, to a Panic concord in which Venus prevails. From Phoebe to Phoebus, from Phoebus to Bacchus, from Bacchus to Venus, is not for a mythologer very far. Yet in another sense it is all the way.

What vouches for the efficacy of rite, says anthropology, is myth. And in the unexpressed presence of Bacchus among the gods named in Shakespeare's play, a mythic validity is apparently sought: a revelation of the healing mystery that must yet remain concealed; some uttering of the ineffable. But what makes such mythologizing good is the poet's ability to find a style of language that enacts, as well as all but names, the mystery in question.

His action is metamorphosis, and accordingly Shakespeare makes his style busy with a continual change. It ranges metrically and varies in diction as no other pastoral comedy quite does. One has only to recall some possible juxtapositions, such as Lysander and Puck on love:

So quick bright things come to confusion. (I. i. 149)

The man shall have his mare again, and all shall be well.
(III. ii. 463)

or Bottom on his dream and Theseus on imagination; or even 'Night and silence . . . who is here?' and 'On the dank and dirty ground' in the same speech of Puck's (II. ii. 78, 83). The more striking or jarring these are, the more remarkable that sense of harmony which the play as a whole still conveys. The best of the blank verse and comic prose by its sophistication confirms the conscious rusticity of Puck's couplets, the *naïveté* of the spells and fairy songs, and the doggerel of Pyramus and Thisbe.

It is difficult to enjoy most Elizabethan mock rusticity. But with the pastoral taste for flexibility of tone in mind one can glimpse its appeal as a poetic *sprezzatura*. And Shakespeare displays here all that flexibility and fluency of voice that Spenser tries for in the *Shepheardes Calender* but is too much the preacher and too little the mime to carry off. 'For Bacchus fruit is frend to Phoebus wise' indeed. But as Milton says in the sixth elegy, Bacchus loves poetry as much as poetry loves Bacchus. And in the end it is the vigour of the style that matters, even in mythology.

As a mythologer Shakespeare says what he does, that chastity is to be reconciled to becoming pleasure: and as a stylist he does what he says by making language and plot agree in enacting that metamorphosis. One must be satisfied with this either aesthetically, it seems, or not at all. In a sense nothing is ever changed by poetic language. On the other hand it can make all things seem possible. This is the difference in humanistic sensibility between Shakespeare and Jonson, both of whose comic styles are superbly mimetic. While in the *Alchemist* or *Bartholomew Fair* all is revealed and given definition, nothing is changed or made to seem newly possible— as it is here or in *As You Like It* or *The Tempest*. Where Jonson has wit, Shakespeare, as Dryden says, has soul.

But beyond the suggestive magic of his mythologizing there remains a final satisfaction to be taken in his pastoral use of language. And this is in the sceptical self-consciousness that plays over it.

(iii) *A Rite of Art*

What is celebrated in *A Midsummer-Night's Dream* is finally the poet's art itself—a certain aesthetic perception of love and language, Platonically conceived, as the agents of a courtly culture. The title word 'dream' accordingly serves as a metaphor for the poetic fiction, the play itself, as in Puck's epilogue:

> If we shadows have offended,
> Think but this, and all is mended,
> That you have but slumbered here,
> While these visions did appear.
> And this weak and idle theme,
> No more yielding than a dream,
> Gentles, do not reprehend. (v. i. 422–8)

Right to the last line *serio ludere* is maintained. Then it is to the audience that the action of dreaming is imputed.

Had Shakespeare written ten years earlier his young lovers and 'rude mechanicals' would have been nymphs and shepherds, more and less clownish, and his title *Love's Metamorphosis*. What he writes is still a pastoral fiction, and as the fourth act gives place to the fifth one knows that there has been no dream, only the play. One knows that Shakespeare knows this and that in calling what happens to Titania or the lovers indifferently 'vision' and 'dream' he is ambiguous for the sake of playful mystification.

Serio ludere determines his stagecraft when he lays the young lovers asleep during the scene in Titania's bower, and again when he lays Bottom asleep while Oberon and Titania 'rock the ground' in dance to fairy music. Whether or not what transpires are dreams, they are evidently images of concord, Bacchus and Apollo reconciled. And so far as they come true in the marriages being celebrated on and offstage, they are prophetic images.

The young lovers, and Titania and Bottom, do not actually dream at all, even in the story. They suffer a trick of Cupid, an erotic transfiguration in the garden of Diana, a pastoral *raptio*. A good deal of doctoral ink has been spent disapproving of these ecstasies of fancy, but according to Platonic theory they can occur in any of six other forms of *vacatio* than sleep—including swoon, solitude, and philosophic or poetic inspiration. And while not all such inner experiences are of divine origin, any decline in the life of the body and the reason, says Ficino, favours an intellectual union with the divine. A 'dream' of any sort may or may not be prophetic, and is always the more enigmatic in that the mind that interprets must be separate from the soul that prophesies.[1]

With this sort of lore in mind, one can see Shakespeare humorously turning round the riddle of his *raptio* and *remeatio*, folly and wisdom. A divinely inspired 'dream' is given only to those who rise above their human limitations while awake, so who is finally to say whose dreaming is the truest form of waking?

---

[1] Ficino, i. 292–5 (*Theologia Platonica*). Cf. Kristeller, *Philosophy of M. Ficino*, pp. 312–13.

As if to ensure this ambiguity he gives the young lovers, awakened by Theseus and his hunting party, a delightful Platonizing quartet, reminiscent in its sceptic mysticism of the *Theatetus* (158D):

> Are you sure
> That we are awake? It seems to me,
> That yet we sleep, we dream. (IV. i. 191-3)

The advance of Shakespeare's command of *serio ludere* from Proteus and the Duke in the *Two Gentlemen* to Demetrius and Theseus here is considerable. Then follows Bottom's great comic esoteric solo:

> I have had a most rare vision. I have had a dream—past the wit of man to say what dream it was. Man is but an ass, if he go about to expound this dream. ... Methought I was—there is no man can tell what. ... Methought I was, and methought I had—but man is but a patched fool, if he will offer to say what methought I had. The eye of man hath not heard, the ear of man hath not seen, man's hand is not able to taste, his tongue to conceive, nor his heart to report, what my dream was. ... (IV. i. 203-13)

It hardly seems necessary to ask about the technical meaning of 'dream' here, whether *somnium*, *visio*, or *oraculum*. Macrobius may be invoked, as for Jonson's more doctrinaire *Vision of Delight*, but Chaucer would do as well. For even Macrobius, after classifying dreams systematically, admits that his particular instance, the *somnium Scipionis*, actually falls into all three classes of significant prophecy—as does the 'dream' that Shakespeare visits upon his audience. And the larger question whether Shakespeare's 'dream' (*narratio fabulosa*) belongs with the decent and true or false and monstrous remains equally ambiguous by reason of the esoteric rule of denying a true interpretation to the vulgar.[1]

A more revealing question is why Bottom—hardly a lunatic, a lover, or a poet—should be vouchsafed a dream of any sort, let alone one suitable to be sung at the death and rebirth of Thisbe in the

---

[1] Macrobius, *Somnium Scipionis*, I. iii. 12: 'Hoc ergo, quod Scipio vidisse se retulit, et illa tria quae sola probabilia sunt genera principalitatis amplectitur et omnes ipsius somnii species attingit': The dream which Scipio reports that he saw embraces the three reliable types . . . and also has to do with all five varieties of enigmatic dream (trans. W. Stahl). Cf. *Orphica*, p. 101 (Hymn to the Divinity of Dreams [*ONEIPOY*]).

flames of heavenly love (IV. i. 218). The answer, presumably, is that like Plato's Ion, Bottom is an actor, a rhapsode, and so a lunatic, a lover, and a poet all in one; a travesty of the whole man who stands like Armado at the centre of a pastoral comedy.[1]

And Bottom being a figure in a conscious fiction, the point of the humour is that the audience may or may not be witnessing a scene enigmatic, prophetic, or oracular in the manner of inspired dreams; an ancestor, priest, or god, as Macrobius says, speaking about the soul.[2] Shakespeare's comedy is all in the may-or-may-not, the metamorphosis of wise and foolish, the putting of the hierophantic into the inarticulate.

What connects dream lore with pastoralism is the same tradition of divine wisdom found in foolish fables which Shakespeare invokes throughout; and finally and most 'obscenely' in the fable of Pyramus and Thisbe, the silliest stuff that ever Hippolyta heard (V. i. 209). He makes this connection perfectly clear at the opening of the last movement of the play in the exchange between Theseus and Hippolyta on 'that these lovers speak of' (v. i. 1):

> More strange than true. I never may believe
> These antic fables, nor these fairy toys.
> Lovers and madmen have such seething brains,
> Such shaping fantasies, that apprehend
> More than cool reason ever comprehends.
> The lunatic, the lover, and the poet
> Are of imagination all compact. (v. i. 2–8)

The rehearsal of the familiar humanistic question of the value of fables effectively draws the pastoral themes of love and poetry, myth and language together and makes the play more completely the subject of itself.

Theseus' speech is justly regarded as crucial; and certainly as a

---

[1] Cf. Plato, *Ion*, 533D–535, where Socrates defines inspiration in Bacchic terms as the taking away of a poet or rhapsode's mind by a god who uses him as a minister. Also Cicero, *De Natura Deorum*, I. xxviii (on Q. Catullus and the actor Roscius); *De Divinatione*, I. xxxvi, II. xxxii, where Midas, Plato, and Roscius are cited as instances of greatness divined prophetically from omens, and the mystical view of prophecy is balanced against the sceptical.

[2] Macrobius, *Somnium Scipionis*, I. iii. 8.

character—if that is the word for it—he now comes into his own, mending his earlier ways. But how, with the sober brand of wisdom still imputed to him, he can ever embody the whole ethos of this play is less easy to see. The importance lies, not in character, but in the mode of Shakespeare's language: a style in which as Hermia says, 'everything is double' (IV. i. 189): nothing may be taken simply for what it seems to mean; all is esemplastic verbal play; Eros, Metamorphosis, Logos. The very phrase 'antic fables' conceitedly sums the matter up. Are they, as Theseus seems to say, foolish; or do they, as Hippolyta suggests, contain an antique wisdom, the *veterum sapientia*?

No audience familiar with what passes for literary criticism in the Renaissance would expect to take sides in this exchange. Nobody is being put right about the poetic imagination, least of all Hippolyta—this is her wedding day. What Shakespeare cleverly rehearses is a known paradox, the very one which makes Ovid and all mythology presentable, as Jonson's alchemist well knows:

> Was not all the knowledge
> Of the Egyptians writ in mystic symbols?
> Speak not the Scriptures oft in parables?
> Are not the choicest fables of the poets,
> That were the fountains and first springs of wisdom,
> Wrapt in perplexed allegories?
>
> (*The Alchemist*, II. iii. 210–15)

This is a venerable answer to the charge that poetry is idle feigning. 'Moving is of a higher degree than teaching', says Sidney, meaning that the inspired imagination somehow tells a higher truth than 'cool reason' alone. And if Theseus is taken straight when he includes the lover and the poet in his critique of madness, then he must be taken to condemn the best received theory of the day. Where would his great good sense be then?

It is the telestic theory that Sidney adapts to English literary usage in the *Defense of Poesy* and that Chapman, Jonson, and many lesser voices all echo: the superiority of heaven-sent madness to mere reason. The ability to rage aright is represented by Plato as a mystical initiation proper to philosopher or poet—Bacchic mania leading to Apolline prophecy. And Ficino several times expounds the divine *furori* of the *Phaedrus* and once pays Lorenzo the highest of compliments by saying that, like Orpheus and David, he is possessed of all four simultaneously.[1]

Shakespeare simply fools with this to the top of his bent. He turns from the love mystery he has just rehearsed and invites his audience to enjoy a bravura display of enigmatic scepticism:

> Theseus: Such tricks hath strong imagination,
> That, if it would but apprehend some joy,
> It comprehends some bringer of that joy;
> Or in the night, imagining some fear,
> How easy is a bush supposed a bear!
> Hippolyta: But all the story of the night told over,
> And all their minds transfigured so together,
> More witnesseth than fancy's images,
> And grows to something of great constancy . . .
> But, howsoever, strange and admirable.
>
> (v. i. 18–27)

Like Oberon and Titania, Theseus and Hippolyta are balanced against each other and against themselves. He is the erotic demigod of Ovid tempered on the more austere model of Plutarch and Chaucer; she owes more to the visionary aestheticism of Felismena in the *Diana* than to the brazen Amazons of tradition.[2] Their pro and con never makes clear what 'these lovers speak of'. And Theseus' scepticism may be an esoteric pose, denying the existence of divine secrets in dreams even to his betrothed. Compare Chaunticleer's misogynic treatment of Pertelote (*Canterbury Tales*, vii. 3151 ff.). Knowing what it hears and sees, an audience is left with the mystery and the poet's sleight-of-hand; as witty an enactment of the esoteric as a connoisseur of pastoral ellipsis could ask for.

With the finale of the *Dream* it is evident that Shakespeare has arrived at his early mastery of the pastoral-comical, a complete and

---

[1] *Phaedrus*, 244–65; Ficino, i. 927 (*Epistolae*); cf. I. 612 (*Epistolae*), ii. 1364–5 (*In Phaedrum*). Also W. Rossky, 'Imagination in the English Renaissance: Psychology and Poetic', *Studies in the Renaissance*, v (1958), 64–6.

[2] Bullough, i. 368; C. T. Wright, 'The Amazons in English Literature', *Studies in Philology*, xxxvii (1940), 456.

original autonomy within the traditional mode. For the first time he achieves a resolution of the pastoral rhythm that is neither inept nor deliberately lame. To do this he resorts, as so often afterwards, to the play within the play, interposing a stage audience of courtiers and lovers between the theatre audience and the poetic fiction so as to induce a certain Platonizing consciousness of self.

I take it to be the final turn of his humour that the fable of Pyramus and Thisbe, for all its burlesque, retains a putative value as love mystery:

> Theseus: How shall we find the concord of this discord?
> Philostrate: A play there is, my lord, some ten words long.
>
> (v. i. 60–1)

As a mock-tragic version of 'the story of the night', Diana reconciled to Venus, it recapitulates the pastoral *raptio*. And the distance between its ludicrous style and its esoteric sense as allegory measures how far Shakespeare is able to carry the art of *serio ludere* without losing coherence:

> If we offend, it is with our good will. (v. i. 108)

To be an initiate is to know oneself.

There is little doubt that the audience for pastoral would appreciate this. Shakespeare certainly prepares one carefully. First there is the literary-critical duet on 'antic fables'. Then Philostrate, master of the revels, offers a choice of masques, all fables, and prominent among them the very gospel of the pastoral mystagogues:

> 'The riot of the tipsy Bacchanals,
> Tearing the Thracian singer in their rage.'
>
> (v. i. 48–9)

Theseus observes that this is 'an old device' before he turns to the next offering, another version of poetic sacrifice but more topical:

> 'The thrice three Muses mourning for the death
> Of learning, late deceased in beggary.' (v. i. 52–3)

And perhaps one is meant to think here of the pastoral devices now in use, newly invented by England's answer to Poliziano and Tasso.

After this, when Theseus has chosen the *dulce amarum* or 'very tragical mirth' of Pyramus and Thisbe, it is no surprise to find its foolishness laced with mocking hints of antique wisdom. The question about all poetry of 'theological' allusion from Ovid to Cocteau is: How much more is meant than meets the ear? But this, at its best, remains a rhetorical question. By comparison with a Spenser, a Marlowe, or a Chapman, Shakespeare does little to nudge one meaningly. And most of what he does in Pyramus and Thisbe is inherent in the names and brought out only by the context as a whole. Granted his prior interest is the ludicrous; but he still clearly acknowledges something else with his Moon and Bacchic Lion and mulberry shade (v. i. 147–50).

Pyramus and Thisbe had apparently been even more thoroughly allegorized by the 1590s than Hero and Leander (v. i. 195), and the presence of a mystery in the slow yet sudden turning of the mulberry from white to red was well established. Apart from Ovid, Pliny makes an early and resounding beginning with his 'wisest of trees'; a tradition which lasts through Shakespeare's century in the most important dictionary of natural history before Linnaeus, the *De Stirpium*, as well as in mythography.[1] And Thomas Mouffet, one of Shakespeare's supposed sources, conforms to this tradition with an apt, if doggerel, riddle:

> What cannot love transform itself into?[2]

Mouffet's poem has the unlikely title *The Silkworms and Their Flies*, but Kitty Scoular in her study of Renaissance nature poems confirms that silkworm and mulberry leaf typically represent the turning of love's woes and follies into pleasure.[3]

So the fable of Pyramus and Thisbe, with its mystery of impassioned reason, the foolish wisdom of love, is a rite as proper to a wedding as any. And the stage audience seems to know this, though the mystical truth in fables can never have been more sorely tried

---

[1] Hieronymus Bock [Tragus], *De Stirpium* (Strasburg, 1552), p. 1048.

[2] K. Muir, 'Pyramus and Thisbe: A Study in Shakespeare's Method', *Shakespeare Quarterly*, v (1954), 148.

[3] As in Marino's *Bombice d'amore*, which Drummond translates as *A Daedale of My Death*; Scoular, pp. 46–8.

than by Bottom the Weaver and company. There is a very knowing tone to the gentles' participation in the rite—a great deal more of lion and ass, certainly, than one otherwise knows what to do with. One could not say of this participation, as of nobility's in *Love's Labour's Lost*:

> This is not generous, not gentle, not humble. (v. ii. 626)

The tolerance Cassirer mentions in that connection is now expressed by Theseus:[1]

> The best in this kind are but shadows: and
> the worst are no worse, if imagination amend them.
> (v. i. 210–11)

The once-tyrannical Duke sets too unctuous a tone here for gentleness to be in question. There is a *participation mystique* in the courtly folly of loving.

But one could say that Shakespeare now exploits to the utmost the convention that the truest poetry is the most feigning. Predictably, he rings a change on the sceptical and hierophantic roles formerly taken by Theseus and Hippolyta, and it is she who is now impatient and has to be reminded of the proper mythic humour:

Hippolyta: I am aweary of this moon. Would he would change!
Theseus: It appears, by his small light of discretion, that he is in the wane: but yet, in courtesy, in all reason, we must stay the time. (v. i. 249–53)

What sort of response is impatience with silliness, when the proposition is that folly may be wisdom? And when the Duke's party and Bottom's party have gone to bed, the fairies come back and confirm the efficacy of all such folly, exorcising by their spells the dark side of Diana-Luna-Hecate and inducing the fertility of Venus.

Perhaps the soundest epitome of Shakespeare's pastoral esotericism in this play is, after all, the epilogue—which in an orthodox love rite would be spoken, not by Puck, but by Titania as Venus *noctiluca*, Puck having spoken the prologue as Cupid.[2] The point is that Shakespeare is never orthodox or doctrinaire. His

---

[1] *Platonische Renaissance*, pp. 123–4.
[2] Macrobius, *Saturnalia*, I. viii. 3 (Venus eadem cum Luna).

recourse is rather to the metamorphic power of language itself. And the response he asks for is an answering delight in his linguistic power from the audience's own imagination. Indeed, discussions like the present one would be pointless, but for the reader in most of us who prefers Platonic doctrine, Christian homily, morals, psychology, folklore—a message of any sort—to mere pastoral style.

CONCLUSION

THE LANDSCAPE OF THE MIND

Of forests, and enchantments drear,
Where more is meant than meets the ear.
                MILTON

(i) *Poetic Theology and* Serio Ludere

HOW much need one know to read sixteenth-century pastoral?

In bringing to bear what knowledge one can, one finds the pastoral poets everywhere at an advantage. Their art by its very nature outdoes any doctrine. It is, as the humanists always say, a theology: fundamentally simple, addressed to the pure in heart, lending itself to endless expatiation but never to being shown to be true. Pastoralism is thus in one sense a body of doctrine, as I have argued. Yet in another sense it is just a poetic trick, the voice crying in the wilderness.

To know this trick of style, no poet need master all the related lore. Only a pedant, talking to pedants, resorts to understanding the joke by documenting it. And is the modern reader with his flair for social, moral, and psychological meaning any less pedantic than the medieval, with his tireless allegorizing of the great fables, the *Song of Solomon*, the *Aeneid*? After the songs of Apollo (or Bacchus) the words of Mercury will always be harsh.

In his *Defense of Poesy* (1595) Sidney allows cleverly for this disadvantage of the critic. Of poetic theology as such he says nothing. What he does, by way of peroration, is to assume the Orphic voice and perform a conjuration:

So that since the ever-praiseworthy poesy is full of virtue-breeding delightfulness, and void of no gift that ought to be in the noble name of learning; since the blames laid against it are either false or feeble; since the cause why it is not esteemed in England is the fault of poet-apes, not poets; since, lastly, our tongue is most fit to honor poesy, and to be honored by poesy; I conjure you all that have had the evil luck to read this ink-wasting toy of mine, even in the name of the nine muses, no more to scorn the sacred mysteries of poesy, no more to laugh at the name of 'poets,' as though they were next inheritors to fools, no more to jest at the reverent title of a 'rimer'; but to believe, with Aristotle, that they were the ancient treasurers of the Grecians' divinity; to believe, with Bembus, that they were first bringers-in of all civility; to believe, with Scaliger, that no philosopher's precepts can sooner make you an honest man than the reading of Virgil; to believe, with Clauserus, the translator of Cornutus, that it pleased the heavenly Deity, by Hesiod and Homer, under the veil of fables, to give us all knowledge, logic, rhetoric, philosophy, natural and moral, and *quid non*; to believe, with me, that there are many mysteries contained in poetry, which of purpose were written darkly lest by prophane wits it should be abused; to believe, with Landin, that they are so beloved of the gods that whatsoever they write proceeds of a divine fury; lastly, to believe themselves, when they tell you they will make you immortal by their verses.

This is the summation of his claims for poetry: a rehearsal of the tradition that it preserves the *teletai*.[1]

In alluding to poetic theology Sidney falls, as might be expected, into the style of *serio ludere*, a Lucianic mockery of the mysteries—Liber Pater, Hercules, Momus, Midas, the hearing of cosmic harmony, the seeing of Socratic beauty, the bardic wisdom of Ireland:[2]

Thus doing, your name shall flourish in the printers' shops; thus doing, you shall be of kin to many a poetical preface; thus doing, you shall be most fair, most rich, most wise, most all; you shall dwell upon superlatives. Thus doing, though you be *libertino patre natus*, you shall sodeinly grow *Herculea proles*, *Si quid mea carmina possunt*. Thus doing, your soul shall be placed with Dante's Beatrix or Virgil's Anchises. But if (fie of such a but) you be born so near the dull-making cataract of Nilus that you cannot hear the planet-like music of poetry, if you

[1] Cf. Aristotle, *Metaphysics*, 982; Boccaccio, *Genealogia*, XIV. viii; J. C. Scaliger, *Poetics*, III. xix; C. Clauser, trans., L. A. Cornutus, *De Natura Deorum Gentilium* (Basle, 1543), Preface, also under Phurnutus, *Poeticarum Fabularum Allegoriis*, *Speculatio* in Hyginus (ed. Micyllus); C. Landino, ed., Dante Alighieri, *Divina commedia* (Florence, 1481), Prol., vii; E. S. Schuckburgh, ed., *Apologie For Poetrie* (Cambridge, 1891), pp. 172–6; G. Shepherd, ed., *Apology For Poetry* (London, 1965), pp. 235–7. Cornutus on the god Comus (ed. Micyllus, p. 170) may be one of Milton's mythographic sources.

[2] Cf. Lucian, *The True History*, i. 7; Horace, *Sermones*, I. vi. 5; *Odes*, I. xii. 21–5; IV. viii. 29–34; xv. 25–32; *Epodes*, vi. 14; Virgil, *Aeneid*, ix. 446; Cicero, *De Republica*, VI. xviii (Somnium Scipionis); Pliny, *Historia Naturalis*, VI. xxv; XXXVI. iv; Hesiod, *Theogony*, l. 214; Ovid, *Metamorphoses*, XI. 92; Shakespeare, *A Midsummer-Night's Dream*, IV. i; *As You Like It*, III. ii. 176–7; Jonson, *Poetaster*, Apologetical Dialogue, l. 263. The sentence in which Sidney brings together echoes of Lucian, Horace, and Virgil is worthy of Joyce.

have so earth-creeping a mind that it cannot lift itself up to look to the sky of poetry, or rather, by a certain rustical disdain, will become such a mome as to be a Momus of poetry; then, though I will not wish unto you, the ass's ears of Midas, nor to be driven by a poet's verses (as Bubonax was) to hang himself, nor to be rimed to death, as is said to be done in Ireland; yet thus much curse I must send you, in the behalf of all poets, that while you live, you live in love, and never get favor for lacking skill of a sonnet, and, when you die, your memory die from the earth for want of an epitaph.

The tone of this mythologizing is burlesque Horatian, the opposite end of the scale from the praise of poetry in, say, 'Bards of Passion, bards of mirth'. But are the gods ever mocked?

Why will this conjurer not wish us a Midas or an Irish bard? Why, if not because they, like all Orphic initiates, do hear the mysteries in poetry but are sworn not to reveal them? Sidney's conjuring is facetious. So, if we wish, we may take it for a meaningless last flourish in a pseudo-classical oration such as the *Praise of Folly*.[1] But dost thou think, gentle reader, because there are cakes and ale there shall be no more virtue?

So familiar a passage of Elizabethan criticism is hardly to be understood without a knowledge of the *facetiae* proper to all esoteric writing, and especially to pastoral. But can one air this knowledge without being a solemn pedant? On the other hand, can one deny its importance to poetry without being a philistine, one of the uninitiated, a non-reader?

(ii) *Pastoral Style and Platonic Doctrine*

The more pastoral the poem, the less demonstrable its secret wisdom. In all the anthology there is no more orthodox, yet no more elusive lyric than Marlowe's *Passionate Shepherd to His Love*. With its ageless invitation to pleasure and delight, the opening stanza typifies the erotic duplicity of the shepherd's life:

> Come live with me, and be my love,
> And we will all the pleasures prove,

[1] Cf. M. Poirier, 'Sidney's Influence Upon *A Midsummer-Night's Dream*', *Studies in Philology*, xliv (1947), 488.

> That valleys, groves, hills and fields,
> Woods, or steepie mountain yields.

The very syntax does what pastoralism always seeks to do: predicate its longing as a vision of natural landscape.

This sentimental erotic device is of course to be found as readily in Virgil or in Hemingway:

> 'I don't want you to do it if you feel that way.'
> The girl stood up and walked to the end of the station. Across, on the other side, were fields of grain and trees along the banks of the Ebro. Far away, beyond the river were mountains. The shadow of a cloud moved across the fields of grain and she saw the river through the trees.
> 'And we could have all this,' she said. (*Hills Like White Elephants*)

What is peculiar to Marlowe and his age is the doctrinaire use to which the allegory of landscape is put. In Hemingway, the movement of the mind's eye over details of landscape is not an ascent of the soul. In Marlowe, though hardly translatable into Platonism, the allegory is not to be understood without it.

Pastoral mythology is made to suggest at once both the perceptions of the senses and the concepts of the soul, delight in the Many and vision of the One, or vice versa. When love speaks, the voice of all the gods, Bacchus-Apollo and Venus in particular, as usual makes heaven drowsy. A seduction poem is offered as a prayer to the Eternal Beauty.

To speak a soul language that does not deny sensuous enjoyment of the world is an ambition shared but not often realized by Marlowe's contemporaries. At mid-century, Hoby already has difficulty Englishing Castiglione's prose poem on the scale of love in the *Cortegiano*. And a generation later Spenser, in the *Hymne of Heavenly Beautie*, fails signally in a similar attempt:[1]

> The meanes therefore which unto us is lent
> Him to behold, is on his workes to looke,
> Which he hath made in beauty excellent . . .

---

[1] I owe these instances to G. Armour Craig.

Thence gathering plumes of perfect speculation,
To impe the wings of thy high flying mynd,
Mount up aloft though heavenly contemplation,
From this darke world, whose damps the soule do blynd. . . .

(ll. 127–9, 133–7)

The mystery of the relation of earthly to heavenly beauty finds
expression here only as a clumsy self-contradiction.

Success in finding a style proper to the erotic whole man—
vielheitliche Einheit: 'blood, imagination, intellect running together'—
seems to have depended either on a high degree of musical ab-
straction, as in Castiglione's Italian, or else on pastoralism, an
understood and long-refined language of sensuous idealism in the
mouth of a Platonizing theologian:

Now lay those sorrowful complaints aside,
And having all your heads with girland crownd,
Helpe me mine owne loves prayses to resound,
Ne let the same of any be envide:
So Orpheus did for his owne bride,
So I unto my selfe alone will sing,
The woods shall to me answer and my Eccho ring.

(*Epithalamion*, ll. 12–18)

Harmonia est discordia concors.[1] This is the way of Spenser at his best,
and of Marlowe in the *Passionate Shepherd*. How far the Orphic voice
takes them is well enough recognized. But by exactly what means,
technically speaking, it is hard for a modern to say.

The Marlowe touch in an otherwise anonymous pastoral lyric is
proleptic: superlative anticipation brought by an impassioned act of
will out of the future and on to the verge of present enjoyment. It
is a touch common to the best passages he wrote for Tamburlaine,
Faustus, Barabas, Gaveston—a rhetorical device equally well
adapted to uttering the pan-erotic soul-world of heroic Neo-
Platonism. But in the *Passionate Shepherd* his main recourse is to
orthodox pastoral language itself.

This, like Neo-Platonism, is no more than classical allusion

---

[1] Harmony is the concordance of discord—F. Gafurius, *De Harmonia Musicorum Instrumentorum*, 1518, frontispiece, cited in Wind, *Pagan Mysteries*, p. 81, q.v.

understood in a certain way. And here it is classical allusion at its
most banal; myrtle for Venus in the third stanza, ivy for Bacchus
in the fifth. No subsequent stanza matches the first for richness of
suggestion or unity of tone. The assumption seems to be that, once
found, the magic voice cannot fail until, like the head singing in
the Hebrus, it passes out of earshot. But simply by refusing to
understand this allusive language in the assumed way, a rival poet
such as Ralegh can expose the peril of its balance between the
purest poetry and the merest doctrine. Witness the *Nymph's Reply
to the Shepherd.*

(iii) *Wit and Mythopoeia*

Ralegh and Donne in their answers to Marlowe both imply that
his recourse is to an old device, now outworn. His doing-power
derives from a mythic element in language which is *passé*. His
singing voice has no range of tone. Thus Ralegh, ignoring the
understood Platonism of all such mythopoeia, carps wittily at an
imputed libertinism:

> Thy gowns, thy shoes, thy beds of roses,
> Thy cap, thy kirtle, and thy posies,
> Soon break, soon wither, soon forgotten;
> In folly ripe, in reason rotten. (ll. 13–16)

So much for the antique wisdom of pastoral folly. The trick is to
take the Orphic sceptically for the language of pagan naturalism;
to make Marlowe with his *serio ludere* sound both naïve and disingenuous—an old-fashioned Platonizing mythologer, and a seducer
to boot.

Ralegh's achievement is in its way more remarkable than
Marlowe's. As with Wyatt earlier in the century, one wonders how
well he understood what he was doing with traditional poetic
discourse. He gives a whole new turn to an old style, replacing
aesthetic mythopoeia with a moral language of paradox. Yet all the
while he relies on pastoralism, no longer as a theology but as some

other sort of literary convention. The shift is one of those 'un-maskings of previous symbolisms' by which the changes in a culture are marked.

But just as one may wonder whether in the Sixth Book of the *Faerie Queene* the heroic comprehends the pastoral or the pastoral the heroic, so here one may ask if Marlowe's limpid song does not comprehend even Ralegh's sententious naturalism. After all, could any language be more mockingly aware of its own limitations, more consciously perfunctory than Marlowe's? And Ralegh knew this. His witty renunciation of pastoralism is not radical.

Donne, in *The Bait*, also takes the pastoral convention—now piscatorial for emphasis—as a way of talking well about something other than the love of beauty. He turns the erotic prayer, by which Marlowe celebrates a soul world ever more about to be, into a rakish and personal intellectual compliment:

> There will the river whispering run,
> Warmed by thy eyes, more than the sun,
> And there th' enamoured fish will stray,
> Begging themselves they may betray. (ll. 5–8)

If you understand, says Donne, you will be flattered by the very fact of my addressing you so wittily. Rites may change, myths may come and go, but the need to be an initiate is never ending.

Yet is the virtue of even this sophistication of the pastoral mode all in its insinuating tone and not at all in the mythos of a universal theism?

Donne, who elsewhere mocks the Platonists, certainly knew more mystic doctrine than Marlowe or Ralegh. Hence, perhaps, his recourse to the piscatorial. Like the bucolic, the piscatorial owes its provenance to Orphism. Through the *Argonautica* and the *Dionysiaca*, the associations of Orpheus with the water are immemorial. Fishermen who are fishers of men play a part in the Bacchic rite of initiation, as pictured in the Villa Farnesina at Rome, or hinted at in *Lycidas*:

> And, O ye dolphins, waft the hapless youth. (l. 164)

And with Christianity, Orpheus comes to figure on the second-century sarcophagus from Ostia and in the Domitilla catacomb as both a shepherd and a fisherman.[1]

At that stage of theological history the Orphic is apparently the exoteric aspect of the hidden god of the Christians. But it is Orpheus the fisher, not the shepherd, who conceals the true magic singer, reincarnate as Jesus. And the practice of not naming him in Christian art persists indefinitely in Europe. After Claudian, Macrobius, Boethius, and Nonnus, it becomes a convention of mythological writing.[2]

Piscatorial poetry, the voice of Orpheus the fisher, could thus be said to be more peculiarly Christian even than the bucolic. And Donne's pagan and licentious manner in *The Bait* may be only a mask for the Christian and mystical. His pastoral wit, even more than Shakespeare's, is all in the may-or-may-not.

Two relics of poetic theology help to bring the orthodoxy of his esotericism to light. One is a phallic fresco, found in the brothel at Pompeii, which represents a girl, possibly Venus, angling with the help of Cupid. The other is the pious epitaph of a second-century Bishop of Hieropolis, in Phrygia, concerning the fish caught by the Virgin Mary:

. . . I am a disciple of a holy shepherd / who feeds flocks of sheep on mountains and plains, / who has great eyes that oversee everything. / It is he who has taught me the true writings . . .

Faith however always went ahead and set before me as food / a fish from a fountain, a huge one, a clean one, / which a holy virgin has caught.

This she gave to the friends ever to eat as food, / having good wine, and offering it watered, together with bread: Whoever can understand this, let him pray for Aberkios . . .[3]

---

[1] R. Eisler, *Orpheus the Fisher* (London, 1921), pp. 59, 271–7, 284–96.

[2] Cf. Chaucer, *Boece*, iii, metre 12; *Canterbury Tales* (ed. Robinson), I. 1163–8 (*Knightes Tale*); Robertson, pp. 106–7 n. For Chaucer, as for Boethius, Orpheus signifies the power of love over reason: 'Who shal yeve a lovere any lawe?' Robertson suggests that to follow Orpheus is to fail to follow the 'true Orpheus', Jesus Christ. But is Chaucer's mythological language as discriminate as this? And does he not know as well as Poliziano or Shakespeare that blind love may be wiser than rational vision?

[3] Eisler, pp. 249–70.

Donne, like any Renaissance pastoralist, seeks 'une impossible conciliation entre la pureté et la volupté, entre la courtoisie et le naturalisme antique'.[1] But, like Ralegh, he brings a new verbal critique to bear upon the mythic propensity of his language—a revision that all the best modernist critics, including the poet of the *Waste Land*, urge us to admire.

The Bait is not the best of the *Songs and Sonnets*. Perhaps it is unworthy of our Poet. Most readers, I suppose, prefer the *Good Morrow*. But without a knowledge of pastoral tradition, who can say he understands even this historic, self-justifying stanza:

> I wonder by my troth, what thou and I
> Did, till we loved? Were we not weaned till then?
> But sucked on country pleasures, childishly?
> Or snorted we in the seven sleeper's den?
> 'Twas so; but this all pleasure's fancies be.
> If ever any beauty I did see,
> Which I desired and got, 'twas but a dream of thee.

The shepherd's life, the idyll of childhood, contemplative retreat, the divinity of dreams, virtue and pleasure reconciled—these pastoral themes are from earliest times the very grounds for poetic 'ambiguity' or 'wit'.

(iv) *Ellipsis and Enigma*

The fascination of pastoral language is the difficulty of coming to a just appreciation of what the poet does not say. Consider that classic fragment

Et in Arcadia ego,

whose author long since earned his pseudonymity. Leslie and Taylor in their life of Reynolds tell the story of Johnson asking what it can possibly mean on a tombstone. Reynolds, in defence of his painting, replies that at least the king had understood very well that it means 'Death is even in Arcadia'. Now Panofsky in his

---

[1] H. Bénac, 'Humanité de la pastorale', *Lettres d'humanité*, v (1946), 243: an impossible reconciliation of purity and pleasure, of courtesy and antique naturalism.

essay on this inscription repeats the story as if at Johnson's expense.[1] But since the phrase in question is pastoral, doubt must remain whether the doctor was outdone as a critic by George III.

Johnson was no lover of pastoral but at least he knew what he did not like. Where there is leisure for equivocation there is little grief. And pastoral is a sort of loose metaphysical style, yoking not by violence but elision. Panofsky infers, perhaps too readily, that any one sense of the inscription excludes any other. The art of it is that more than one sense is carried at the same time: a *floreat* as well as a *memento mori*, as in *Lycidas*.

There is nothing like the topic of death in youth for bringing out the Orphic in a poet's voice in any age:

> If I should die, think only this of me:
> That there's some corner of a foreign field
> That is for ever England.
>
> (Rupert Brooke, *The Soldier*, ll. 1–3)

As with all enigma, one is left like Johnson wondering exactly what can be meant.

The heroic counterpart of *Et in Arcadia ego* is

> Time . . . must have a stop. (1 *Henry IV*, v. iv. 82–3)

Is this a mortal premonition or a promise of eternity? The only satisfaction is that it may be either or both. Context rarely makes as much difference in such cases as one might suppose. Consider the Horatian ode on Cleopatra's fall:

> Nunc est bibendum, nunc pede libero.[2] (Horace, *Odes*, 1. xxxvii)

As Sidney is wise enough to allow, who can say for sure whether or not Liber Pater, cult hero of the Ptolemies, lies concealed in such a line? Even in the case of Donne, the ground that a reading knowledge of pastoral leads on to is not so much 'ambiguity' or 'wit' as ellipsis—that which is not said at all, the non-articulation of experience.

---

[1] C. R. Leslie and T. Taylor, *Life and Times of Sir Joshua Reynolds* (London, 1865), i. 325. Cf. Panofsky, *Meaning in the Visual Arts*, p. 295. The painting in question is the double portrait of Mrs. Bouverie and Mrs. Crewe.

[2] Now is the time to drink and [dance] with foot set free [beating the ground].

(v) Who goes with Fergus? *and Ambiguity*

The Orphic voice is heard in every age of English poetry, from 'Whan that April' to the song from the *Countess Cathleen* that haunted Stephen Dedalus. In *Marriage à La Mode* or the *Rape of the Lock* the ludic becomes almost everything and the theological almost nothing. But with Blake and Wordsworth theologizing again breaks out. In the seventeenth century, it is said, the course of the best modern poetry is set by those who already take new bearings. But in Donne, Jonson, and Marvell, as well as in Milton, pastoralism persists. The question is, Does it any longer matter?

Here the bias of modernist criticism is the reverse of that of Northrop Frye. Where the one is so taken with the mythic as to ignore the difference between pastoral and New Comedy, the other is not interested in mythology as a language at all. Empson, for instance, usually brings out an ambiguity in the pastoral poem that is by definition verbal. Yet the sense of it is usually mythological—even in free modern versions such as Yeats's, for whom the view of pastoral language given here would have little novelty.

Who Goes with Fergus? (1893) makes an interesting case in point. The myth it names is Gaelic, but its logic is that of the Greek theology as read by a Platonist:

> Who will go drive with Fergus now,
> And pierce the deep wood's woven shade,
> And dance upon the level shore?
> Young man, lift up your russet brow,
> And lift your tender eyelids, maid,
> And brood on hopes and fear no more.
>
> And no more turn aside and brood
> Upon love's bitter mystery;
> For Fergus rules the brazen cars,
> And rules the shadows of the wood,
> And the white breast of the dim sea
> And all dishevelled wandering stars.

Empson reads this as a statement which, by contradicting itself or being irrelevant, says nothing:

. . . so that the reader is forced to invent statements of his own and they are liable to conflict with one another.[1]

This is an ingenious, up-to-date way of reading the poem—a search for complexity. But it overlooks the Orphic preference for the simple.

The two lives of Fergus are the active or worldly, and the contemplative or otherworldly to which he turned after opening the Druid's bag of dreams. See *Fergus and the Druid*. And as Empson says, the first stanza leaves it uncertain whether the call is to one or the other—though 'pierce', 'dance', 'lift up', and 'brood no more' sound like a call to action. But no one who knows he is reading poetic theology should feel 'forced to invent statements of his own'. What such language seeks to do is hold the contraries in harmony while the truth comes—if at all—from somewhere beyond words.

Reading Genesis, one may think Esau should be recompensed or Leah preferred to Rachel, but they are not. In Luke, one may expect Jesus to rebuke Mary when Martha complains, but he does not. And the sense of these and all such models is a preference for the contemplative that yet acknowledges the active and its due. That there are so many such models in Western art, from Cain and Abel to 'Johnny, I hardly knew ye', only makes their mystery seem simpler. Mythological usage leads one to expect Yeats to put his contraries into a meaningful relation, and he does. For once the older language of myth works harder for clarity than the newer language of words as word, not for contradiction but modality.

Empson finds three unresolved meanings in the third line of Yeats's final stanza: Fergus is still an heroic king; he is 'true ruler only of the dim appurtenances of magic dreams'; and he is 'a poet or philosopher or what not who drives some mythological chariot of the Muses'. Here the verbal critic pleasantly deprecates any knowledge of mythology. But a 'sixth type of ambiguity' can be found only by ignoring the sense of 'now' as 'after' that the unfolding mythological sense of the poem calls for—the active put into the contemplative. There comes a point when any temporal ordering

---

[1] *Seven Types of Ambiguity*, p. 176.

of active and contemplative can be abandoned—active becomes contemplative and vice versa; but not yet.

The context is the usual Christian Platonic attempt to compose the divisions of a mind to which the two lives of Fergus seem now of greater and lesser, now of lesser and greater, now of equal, value. As with the judgement of Paris, the ways of hero, lover, and sage seem to diverge. Yet the right sort of passion can turn a young man into a good soldier, a good poet, or better still both. The way of Eros is for the Platonist a way to all experience. 'Make love not war', says the campaign button on the girl in a crash helmet: 'Lloyd George did both', says the old man with the *Guardian* in his pocket.[1]

The mystery—the 'problem' as it is now called—is the brooding mind of the young lover, man or maid. Twice the poet enjoins a turn from brooding: first, it seems, to action; then to a contemplation that comprehends action. Since even the best minds are fated to brood, it is how one broods and on what that matters. Melancholy is saturnian, pathic yet divine.

Mythopoeia calls for a less exclusive understanding of what is meant than the critic with an eye for contradiction or irrelevance allows. The reader who comes to the second stanza and means to see the poem through has to bear the amorous as well as the heroic sense of the first stanza in mind and be ready to compose them in the pastoral manner. Somehow the movement from word to word involves, not rejection, but synthesis such as the death and new life of Orpheus implies.

As a dead religion mythology explains nothing in the way that more rational language seems to do. It only paraphrases itself. But in doing so it expresses the mind at another level than the verbal. This is apparently why a wordmaster like Yeats values it. In the *Autobiographies* he tells of his long search, not for the explanatory sentence but for the 'simplifying image'.

If one asks how different human desires may be composed, how brooding may be a matter of indifference, beyond good and evil,

---

[1] Cartoon by Trog in the London *Observer*, 25 Sept. 1966, p. 36. Cf. Virgil, *Bucolics*, x. 44: 'Nunc insanus amor duri me Martis in armis': Now a mad passion for Mars the rough god of war [keeps] me in [his] arms.

then the answer is that in *Who Goes with Fergus?* Yeats does not say how. All he does is invoke skilfully some ancient myth of composure, a yoking of clarity and the dithyrambic, as in

> For Fergus rules the brazen cars,
> And rules the shadows of the wood.

Since the meaning of a myth always remains a mystery, his words do not explain but only epitomize it.

Empson, with his excellent ear, easily catches the triumph of the first line here. But this is as much an Apolline triumph of the transfigured king as an elegy on his former regality. To an ear attuned to mythology, the transfiguring of Fergus, 'grown nothing, knowing all' (*Fergus and the Druid*), implies reconciliation rather than loss.[1] Hence the thrilling juxtaposition of 'brazen' and 'shadows' which, with the repeating of 'rules', sounds transcendent rather than contradictory. Hence the fact that 'cars' rhymes forward with 'stars'.

Grammatically, these two lines read as clauses in a compound sentence whose fourfold order corresponds to the elements in the cosmos. The effort of the maker of the sentence is to enlarge the context of human action by unifying and, in imitation of the mage, inhabiting all the analogous spheres of life. Mythology as usual assumes the antique cosmos, and the poem is not discretely circular in its contradictions but spiral—'gyre-like', Yeats might say. For all its articulateness, it speaks in a vague, visionary language. Words like 'russet' and 'dishevelled' do the work of stanzas, but all the poet needs is the right name said in the right way. And since the reader, to understand, needs to know about Fergus already, 'statements of his own' are unnecessary.

The mystery that a myth embodies has its verbal counterpart in paradox—a form of contradiction notably absent from what Yeats actually writes. The way to follow up his meaning is to go from the words to the mythology. In this case, does the 'criterion for the

---

[1] Cf. *Richard II*, III. iii. 54, where Bolingbroke is given similar language in which to conciliate as well as challenge the king, putting the political into the elemental, and vice versa.

sixth class' turn out to be 'verbal' at all? One ends needing to know more about Fergus than is within the verbal range of this poet.

(vi) *Wisdom and Folly*

The pastoralist in any poet is that part of him which knows how little of what matters can be said. In English, the early master of the bland, enigmatic style of unjoined paradox that results is Marlowe:

> Nature, that framed us of four elements
> Warring within our breasts for regiment,
> Doth teach us all to have aspiring minds.
> Our souls, whose faculties can comprehend
> The wondrous architecture of the world
> And measure every wandering planet's course,
> Still climbing after knowledge infinite,
> And always moving as the restless spheres,
> Wills us to wear ourselves and never rest,
> Until we reach the ripest fruit of all,
> That perfect bliss and sole felicity,
> The sweet fruition of an earthly crown.
>
> (1 *Tamburlaine*, II. vii. 18–29)

The rhetoric here—though heroic in mood—is a conscious lavishing of otherworldly attributes upon the worldly; naturalism seeking with all the gravity of the tragic to comprehend the life of the soul:

> Do then by dying, what life cannot do.
>
> (Ralegh, *Ocean to Cynthia*, l. 496)

But like the pastoral in the *Passionate Shepherd* or *Who Goes with Fergus?* such rhetoric assumes a looseness of understanding alien to a modern reader. It is in this alienation that he and modernist critics are at one.

It is not difficult to see why, when singling out the modern masters by the criterion of articulateness, Leavis would pass reluctantly over Yeats as one who spent too much of his remarkable power 'outside poetry'.[1] The work of *Scrutiny* has been to put the

[1] F. R. Leavis, *New Bearings in English Poetry* (London, 1950), p. 44. For Yeats as

whole of the English anthology to a critique of high seriousness
that it rarely satisfies. Approval being reserved for poetry which is
complex and 'does what it says', pastoral has been more or less
dropped, except as it can be read as something else. For when a
pastoralist puts the complex into the simple, the verbal proof that
he has dealt with complexity usually disappears, and he has to be
taken on trust or not at all. The exception is the metaphysical
idyll.

As a reader I do not foresee 'getting over' Leavis, as a week-end
reviewer would say. But there is a good deal of pastoral poetry I do
not foresee getting over either, simple, elliptical, esoteric as it is.
For better or worse, poetic language has an element of pastoral in it.
Some poets do what they say, but does any poet ever say what he
means?

Part of the function of poetry has always been to sing the un-
sayable, a practice less accessible to a critic's intelligence than one
might wish. No matter how well Milton in *Paradise Lost* verbally
enacts his claim to inspiration, his words will never prove he knows
whereof he speaks:

> Thee Sion and the flowery brooks beneath
> That wash thy hallowed feet, and warbling flow,
> Nightly I visit: nor sometimes forget
> Those other two equalled with me in Fate,
> So were I equalled with them in renown,
> Blind Thamyris and blind Maeonides,
> And Tiresias and Phineus prophets old.
> Then feed on thoughts, that voluntary move
> Harmonious numbers; as the wakeful bird
> Sings darkling, and in shadiest covert hid
> Tunes her nocturnal note. (III. 30–40)

The word 'voluntary' remains an Orphic cypher.

When Scaliger in his chapter on pastoral mentions most of the
pantheon but not Orpheus, is this esotericism or incompetence?
For the critic and teacher esotericism obviously has its drawbacks.

pastoral theologian, cf. F. A. C. Wilson, *W. B. Yeats and Tradition* (London, 1958),
pp. 199–205.

To go with Fergus one must admit, like any esoteric, that more may be known than can be said, and that to be taught is to be reminded of what one already knows. 'I teach not,' says Montaigne with his customary good sense, 'I tell' (*Essais*, III. ii).

No one ever came to terms with pastoralism who did not know that his thought and language can with profit be turned round upon themselves: death as love, Aeneas as false Trojan, Fergus as melancholy sage, folly as wisdom. This is where a pastoral poet runs foul of modernist criticism, with its preference for the serious and complex. When Leavis objects that the moral theme of *Comus* is presented with 'singleminded seriousness' one knows what he means. In Milton as in Spenser there is often, as there seldom is in Jonson, a failure of ludic nerve:

> This way the noise was, if mine ear be true,
> My best guide now; me thought it was the sound
> Of riot and ill managed merriment,
> Such as the jocund flute, or gamesome pipe
> Stirs up among the loose unlettered hinds,
> When for their teeming flocks and granges full
> In wanton dance they praise the bounteous Pan
> And thank the gods amiss. (ll. 170–7)

Single-minded to the point of being prissy. But can any theme presented in pastoral language ever fitly be called *serious*?

The serious is one side of the dialectic that is poetry; the other is the dilettante. And a poet who proposes

> To triumph in victorious dance
> O'er sensual folly and intemperance (ll. 974–5)

has the critic who invokes 'seriousness' at a disadvantage. Not that pastoral poetry is beyond criticism. But what is wrong with the would-be *serio ludere* of *Comus* deserves to be judged by some more fitting canon.

It would be different if pastoralism always made for a worse poetry rather than a better. 'Not that fair field of Enna' (*Paradise Lost*, iv. 268 ff.) is a case in point. There is no denying the change that comes over English poetry during Shakespeare's lifetime, or the virtue of the later styles. But what is the new wit if not the old mythology writ tight and small by men of Donne and Jonson's intelligence? The final vulgarity of modernist criticism is the premiss that one reads such poetry for, as Brooks and Warren would say, 'understanding'. Even Hobbes, for all the rationality of his prose, expects one to ponder the enigma of a monster called Leviathan.

Is poetry the conversation of a wit or the images and music of a magician who knows the right names? It is not a matter of either, but both:

> Again and again . . . myth receives new life and wealth from language, as language does from myth. And this constant interaction . . . attests the unity of the mental principle from which both are sprung, and of which they are simply different expressions.[1]

In the pastoral anthology, *Who Goes with Fergus?* finds its opposite number in Karolin's song from the *Sad Shepherd*, nearly three hundred years older but a better subject for verbal criticism:

> Though I am young, and cannot tell
> Either what Death or Love is well,
> Yet I have heard they both bear darts,
> And both do aim at human hearts:
> And then again, I have been told,
> Love wounds with heat, as Death with cold;
> So that I fear they do but bring
> Extremes to touch, and mean one thing.
>
> As in a ruin we it call
> One thing to be blown up or fall;
> Or to our end, like way may have
> By a flash of lightning, or a wave:
> So Love's inflamed shaft or brand
> May kill as soon as Death's cold hand,
> Except Love's fires the virtue have
> To fright the frost out of the grave.

The convention here is logic, not magic. And in view of its para-

---

[1] E. Cassirer, *Language and Myth*, trans. S. Langer (New York, 1946), p. 97.

doxes, one may question the thesis that pastoralism calls for a mythological reading. Is there ever anything that Jonson means that he cannot say?

As usual in his poetry, a world of words stands uninterrupted by the mysteries that mythology implies. What is said is that folly may be wisdom after all, the gospel according to Erasmus. Yet between this perfectly articulate statement and that shifting body of myth, experience, convention, and ideas which it never brings into focus a certain relation is taken for granted. This is undemonstrable but evident. Jonson makes himself the master of words that he is by knowing how very little they can say.

(vii) *Enlightenment*

Pastoralism, as represented here, offers perhaps the least congenial aspect of Renaissance poetry. It could well be ignored, if only the best writers of the age, including the most progressive, did not rely on it—and not merely in their immaturity. In Shakespeare, *As You Like It* is the only mature comedy that answers exactly to this account of the landscape of the mind. Yet it could be shown to accommodate also that crucial development in the setting and tone of the comedies which culminates in *Much Ado About Nothing* and the tragi-comic cry of 'Kill Claudio!' (IV. i. 288).[1]

The future lay with Utopias, not Arcadias; Montaigne, not Tasso. But 'as they liked it' was evidently pastoral, the merest, most gratuitous of modes which, like Shakespeare's stage, appeals to a taste for the arts of language rather than for nature realized. To the very end the model of the *Aminta* remains discernible in his work—as witness *The Tempest*. Pastoralism as in Tasso and an answering primitivism as in Montaigne are there brought together.[2]

Who of that age can now speak to us more immediately, 'as... the living', than Montaigne? Yet where a modern reader might

---

[1] Cf. Cassirer, *Platonische Renaissance*, pp. 124–7.
[2] Cf. F. R. Leavis, *The Common Pursuit* (London, 1952), p. 189; L. Marx, *The Machine in the Garden* (New York, 1964), pp. 34–72.

think him most himself he owes most to pastoralism—as, for instance, in the gentle ridicule of any rule of life but the 'sensible-intellectual' in *De l'expérience*:

The Cirenaique Philosophers are of opinion, that as griefes, so corporall pleasures are more powerfull; and as double, so, more just. There are some (as Aristotle saith) who with a savage kinde of stupidity, will seeme distastefull or squemish of them. Some others I know, that doe it out of ambition. Why renounce they not also breathing? why live they not of their own (que ne vivent-ils pas du leur?), and refuse light, because it commeth of gratuity: and costs them neither invention nor vigor? That Mars, or Pallas, or Mercurie, should nourish them to see, instead of Ceres, Venus, or Bacchus? Will they not seeke for the quadrature of the circle, even upon their wives? I hate that we should be commanded to have our minds in the clouds, whilst our bodies are sitting at the table; yet would I not have the minde to be fastned thereunto, nor wallow upon it, nor lie along thereon, but to apply it selfe and sit at it. Aristippus defended but the body, as if wee had no soule: Zeno embraced but the soule, as if we had no body. Both viciously. Pythagoras (say they) hath followed a Philosophie all in contemplation; Socrates altogether in manners and in action. Plato hath found a mediocrity between both. But they say so by way of discourse. For, the true temperature is found in Socrates; and Plato, is more Socratical then Pythagorical, and it becomes him best. When I dance, I dance; and when I sleepe, I sleepe. And when I am solitarie walking in a faire orchard, if my thoughts have a while entertained themselves with strange occurrences, I doe another while bring them to walke with mee in the orchard, and to be partakers of the pleasure of that solitarinesse and of my selfe. Nature hath like a kinde mother observed this, that such actions as shee for our necessities hath enjoyned unto us, should also be voluptuous unto us. (*Essais*, III. xiii. trans. J. Florio)

Here in the space of a paragraph are the elements and formula of a pastoralism such as Tasso's: Socratic–Platonic compromise, Greek theology, landscape of the mind. Only Montaigne's composition of them is unique.

It may be that the *Essais* are a protean source in which one can find anything one looks for. But more lies behind the words of any great writer than prudential reading will ever discover. Suppose one were to look into the expression 'que ne vivent-ils pas du leur', with its hint of Pico's chameleon man; or better still the allusion to the judgement of Paris in *De l'Institution des enfants*:

Now the tutour, which ought to know, that he should rather seek to fill the mind, and store the will of his disciple, as much, or rather more, with love and affection, than with awe, and reverence unto vertue, may shew and tell him, that Poets follow common humours, making him plainly to perceive, and as it were palpably to feele, that the Gods have rather placed labour and sweat at the entrances, which lead to Venus chambers, than at the doores, that direct to Pallas cabinets. And when he shall perceive his scholler to have a sensible feeling of himselfe, presenting Bradamant, or Angelica before him, as a Mistresse to enjoy, embelished with a naturall, active, generous, and unspotted beautie, not uglie, or Giant-like, but blithe and livelie, in respect of a wanton, soft, affected, and artificiall-flaring beautie; the one attired like unto a young man, coyfed with a bright-shining helmet, the other disguised and drest about the head like unto an impudent harlot, with embroyderies, frizelings, and carcanets of pearles; he will no doubt deeme his owne love to be a man and no woman, if in his choice he differ from that effeminate shepherd of Phrygia. (*Essais*, I. xxv)

Here Montaigne plays enigmatically with the same difficult motif of choice and reconciliation in a landscape that Shakespeare experiments with at the climax of the *Two Gentlemen*. Elsewhere, in *Sur des vers de Virgile*, he rehearses mockingly the very names and phrases by which the pastoral ethos can be identified:

I easily beleeve Plato, who saieth, that easie or hard humours, are a great prejudice unto the mindes goodnesse or badnesse. Socrates had a constant countenance, but light-some and smyling: not frowardly constant, as old Crassus, who was never seene to laugh. Vertue is a pleasant and buxom quality . . .

I know not who could set Pallas and the Muses at oddes with Venus, and make them cold and slow in affecting of love; as for me, I se no Deities that better sute together, nor more endebted one to another. Who-ever shal go about to remove amourous imaginations from the Muses, shall deprive them of the best entertainement they have, and of the noblest subject of their work: and who shall debarre Cupid the service and conversation of Poesie, shall weaken him of his best weapons . . .

The Sciences handle this over finely, with an artificiall manner, and different from the vulgar and naturall forme. My Page makes love, and understands it feelingly; Read Leon Hebraeus or Ficinus unto him; you speake of him, of his thoughts and of his actions, yet understands he nothing what you meane. I nor acknowledge nor discerne in Aristotle, the most part of my ordinary motions. They are clothed with other robes, and shrouded under other vestures, for the use of Academicall schooles. God send them well to speed: but were I of the trade, I would naturalize Arte, as much as they Artize nature. There let us leave Bembo and Equicola.

To conclude, he that could recover or un-besot man, from so scrupulous and verball a superstition, should not much prejudice the world. Our life consisteth partly in folly, and partly in wisedome.

(*Essais*, III. v)

As comprehended here, it is part of that aesthetic Platonic spirit of the age which may be summed up as 'the courtly folly of loving'. Montaigne, whose primitivism was to supplant Italianate pastoralism in the more empirical generations to come, still shares it as an idiom with Tasso and Shakespeare.

Even in Bacon, who best anticipates the Enlightenment, pastoralism finds its echo. In the *Veterum Sapientia* (1609) ethical readings of the poetic theology engage him in earnest—confirming perhaps how uncongenial to him aesthetic Platonic tradition actually was. But in the First Book of the *Advancement of Learning* he concludes with an enigmatic acknowledgement of the mysteries, familiar to the reader of pastoral:

Nevertheless I do not pretend, and I know it will be impossible for me, by any pleading of mine, to reverse the judgement, either of Aesop's cock, that preferred the barley-corn before the gem; or of Midas, that being chosen judge between Apollo, president of the Muses, and Pan, god of the flocks, judged for plenty; or of Paris, that judged for beauty and love against wisdom and power; or of Agrippina, 'occidat matrem, modo imperet' that preferred empire with any condition never so detestable; or of Ulysses, 'qui vetulam praetulit immortalitati', being a figure of those which prefer custom and habit before all excellency; or of a number of the like popular judgements. For these things must continue as they have been: but so will that also continue whereupon learning hath ever relied, and which faileth not: 'Justificata est sapientia a filiis suis.' (I. viii. 7)

Apparently Bacon conceived of this work as a version, in deliberative prose, of pastoral. Seeking a new unity of action and contemplation, theory and practice, he recurs predictably to that mythology of 'Orpheus' theatre' which remains mandatory in any discourse on the good life of the mind at least through Cowley's time:

... Wherein is aptly described the nature and condition of men, who are full of savage and unreclaimed desires, of profit, of lust, of revenge; which as long as they give ear to precepts, to laws, to religion, sweetly touched with eloquence and persuasion of books, of sermons, of harangues, so long is society and peace maintained; but if these instruments be silent, or that sedition and tumult make them not audible, all things dissolve into anarchy and confusion. (*Advancement*, I. vii. 2)

And in the Second Book he rests his case concerning natural philosophy on a line from Virgil's last Eclogue:

If it be truth, *Non canimus surdis, respondent omnia sylvae*; the voice of nature will consent to my argument, whether the voice of man do or not. (II. viii. 4)

Buccinator novi temporis; but no less apt than Boccaccio to read the *Bucolics* as philosophy.

The letter killeth, but the spirit giveth life. It is notable how much of the language of pastoralism persists in Bacon's English prose and how little of the Platonic ethos. Yet in the long view the one turns out to be no less persistent than the other. And I can end with the judicious tribute of a modern man of letters:

As to the Socratic philosophy of love, there is an obvious spiritual tendency in it, inasmuch as it bids the heart turn from the temporal to the eternal; and it does so not by way of an arid logic but by a true discipline of the affections, sublimating erotic passion into a just enthusiasm for all things beautiful and perfect. This is the secret of Platonism, which makes it perennial, so that if it were ever lost as a tradition it would presently be revived as an inspiration. It lives by a poignant sense of eternal values—the beautiful and the good—revealed for a moment in living creatures or in earthly harmonies. Yet who has not felt that this Platonic enthusiasm is somewhat equivocal and vain? Why? Because its renunciation is not radical. In surrendering some particular hope of personal object of passion, it preserves and feeds the passion itself: there is no true catharsis, no liberation, but a sort of substitution and subterfuge, often hypocritical.[1]

For this is equally the secret of pastoralism; so that if it were ever lost as a tradition, it would presently be revived as an inspiration, equivocal and vain as it is.

[1] G. Santayana, *Works* (New York, 1937), x. 178 (*Platonism and the Spiritual Life*).

INDEX

Titles of works cited are as a rule entered only under the author's or compiler's name. Further bibliographical details are given at the first reference in the notes.

patrons of, 134; a figure in a metamorphosis, 142; in Marlowe, as erotic whole man, 155–6; in Ralegh, a mystagogue and seducer, 158; in Donne, a seducer and mystagogue, 159–61.

Sidney, P. (1554–86), *Defense of Poesy*, 153–5 (cited); mentioned, 16, 145, 162; ed. E. S. Shuckburgh, 154 n.; ed. G. Shepherd, 154 n.; *Astrophil and Stella*, 42; *Arcadia*, 81, 139; mentioned, 90.

Silenus, 5, 25, 38, 53, 111, 138.

Silvanus, 53.

Sisson, C. F., *New Readings in Shakespeare*, 117 n.

Smith, G. G., ed., *Elizabethan Critical Essays*, 16 n.

Smith, H., *Elizabethan Poetry*, 7 n., 8, 82 n., 106 n., 113 n.

Snell, B., *Entdeckung des Geistes* (trans. T. G. Rosenmeyer), 10–11 and n.

Social Life, the courtier, 5, 12, 17–18, 40, 43–9, 50–3, 59, 60–1, 67, 70–6 *passim*, 83–7 *passim*, 91–4 *passim*, 98, 101 n., 106–23 *passim*, 128, 141, 147; courtly love, 10, 14, 43, 52, 60, 92; festivity, 13, 34, 38–9, 42, 47, 57, 94, 102, 113–14, 119, 128; topical allusion, 15, 39–40, 53, 58, 112–14, 118, 121; initiation, 15, 28, 38–9, 44, 60, 72–4, 77, 93, 102, 112, 145, 147, 159; patronage, 31, 43, 59, 66, 74, 107, 111, 113, 124, 138; a man's world, 32 n., 41, 43, 54, 149; compliment, 41, 43, 59, 66, 107, 115, 128, 130, 159; 'courtly folly of loving', 51, 86, 149, 174; *sprezzatura*, 51–2, 72, 74, 98, 108, 140; court of Urbino, 50–2, 63; court of Ferrara, 53, 58, 66, 74, 78, 81, 114. Cf. Theatre.

Socrates (470?–399 B.C.), as shepherd, 4, 9–10, 11, 83; Socratic humour, 17–18; Socratic speech, 23–6, 36, 63, 172, 173; and Orpheus, 28–30; dialectic, 32, 33; as satyr, 38–9, 53; homoerotic, 43; shepherd as, 47–8; Bembo as, in *Cortegiano*, 51; on the aesthetic stage, 59; on mythological language, 61; Tasso in, in *Aminta*, 63–4, 75; anticipates pastoral-heroic obverse, 106–7; as patron of the ass, in *Moriae Encomion*, 138; on inspiration, 144 n.; in

Sidney's *Defense*, 154; in Montaigne, 172–3; Santayana on, 175–6. Cf. *Serio ludere*.

Sophocles (496?–406 B.C.), *Oedipus Rex*, 27.

Southampton, H. Wriothesley, second earl of (1573–1624), 90.

Spenser, E. (1552?–1599), *Faerie Queene*, 6, 38, 105, 106, 111, 112, 132 and n., 135, 159; *Shepheardes Calender*, 39, 42 and n. (October, l. 106), 81, 132 n. (April, emblem), 140–1; *Hymne of Heavenly Beauty*, 156 (ll. 127–37); *Epithalamion*, 157 (ll. 12–18); mentioned, 18.

Stevenson, R. L. (1850–94), 'A Gossip on Romance', 61 n.

Stoicism, 34 n.; *ars vivendi*, 64, 106, 108 and n.

Strabo (64? B.C.–A.D. 21?), *Geography*, on the art-for-art's-sake of the Bacchic and Orphic arts, 42 n.

Style, musical, 32, 39; bitter-sweet, 37, 76–7, 121, 148; rustic, 38–9, 74, 140, 155; prophetic, 39–40, 74, 142, 144; travesty, 100, 106, 108, 115–26, 136–40, 144, 147–8, 154–5, 159.

Symbolism, s.v. Allegory.

Symeone, G. (1509–78), *Sententiose imprese*, 110.

Symonds, J. A. (1840–93), *Renaissance in Italy*, 8 and n., 43 n.; 'Orfeo', 31 and n., 43.

Tasso, T. (1544–95), a pastoral poet, 4, 7, 83; a Platonic theologian, 12–14, 45, 48, 55–6, 63–77, 86; apparently alluded to in *AMND*, 15, 147; theory behind his mythologizing, 16; scepticism, 18, 75; his pastoralism in relation to Shakespeare's, 19, 77–8, 81–2, 92, 111, 127; anticipated by Poliziano, 23, 36, 40; anticipated by Plato, 26, 46; his Orphism, 30, 48, 53, 61–77; a poet of the love passion, 43, 44–5; a poet of the inner life, 46, 56–7; his language of landscape, 46–9; a courtier poet, 50–2, 58–9; his mystical sensuality, 54; a poet of the aesthetic stage, 59–60, 95; his relation to Ficino, 59, 62 and n.; his power of language, 61, 67, 74–7; theatrical use of prologue, epilogue, and *intermedi*,

PRINTED IN GREAT BRITAIN
AT THE UNIVERSITY PRESS, OXFORD
BY VIVIAN RIDLER
PRINTER TO THE UNIVERSITY